OXFORD SKILLS WORLD

Reading 6
WITH Writing

Renata Brunner-Jass

OXFORD
UNIVERSITY PRESS

OXFORD
UNIVERSITY PRESS

198 Madison Avenue
New York, NY 10016 USA

Great Clarendon Street, Oxford, OX2 6DP, United Kingdom

Oxford University Press is a department of the University of Oxford.
It furthers the University's objective of excellence in research, scholarship,
and education by publishing worldwide. Oxford is a registered trade
mark of Oxford University Press in the UK and in certain other countries

ISBN: 978 0 19 411356 4 Student Book with Workbook

Printed in China

This book is printed on paper from certified and well-managed sources

ACKNOWLEDGMENTS

*Oxford University Press would like to thank all of the teachers whose opinions helped to
inform this series, and in particular, the following reviewers*: Soo Ah Chung, Hwarang
Elementary School; Marta Juanet, Betania-patmos; Sedef Toksöz Kaykın,
Denizli Pamukkale Unv Egitim Vakfi okullari (PEV Koleji); Jeehee Moon,
T.T.R.; Jacob Rod, WILS Language School; Yuechun Wang, Phoenix City
International School

Cover illustration and main character illustrations by: Shane McGowan/The
Organisation

Back cover photograph: Oxford University Press building/David Fisher

Student Book

Illustrations by: 5W Infographics pp.41, 46, 101; Scott Angle/Carole Newman
& Associates pp.17, 44, 65, 66, 72, 73; Valentina Beloni/MB Artists p.59; EMC
Design pp.50, 51, 60, 83; Peter Francis/MB Artists pp.79, 80; Leslie Harrington
pp.55, 56, John Kurtz p.45; Anthony Lewis/MB Artists pp.11, 30, 38, 43, 57, 71,
81; Julissa Mora p.27; Juan Moreno/MB Artists pp.37, 67, 85; Caroline Romanet/
Advocate Art pp.70, 86; Jomike Tejido/MB Artists p.9; John White/The Neis
Group p.69

*The Publishers would like to thank the following for their kind permission to reproduce
photographs and other copyright material*: 123rf: pp.10 (octopus/Michal
Adamczyk), 24 (girl riding bicycle/Jacek Chabraszewski), 31 (brother and sister
cycling/Jacek Chabraszewski), 35 (close up of compass/Suwat Wongkham),
42 (girl with compass/Alexey Poprotsky), 51 (language dictionaries/
Dmitry Rukhlenko); Alamy: pp.23 (girls in a canoe/Blend-Memento),
40 (orienteering control flag/Robert Matton AB), 84 (man in submarine/
Martin Florin Emmanuel), 87 (man kayaking/Westend61 GmbH); Getty: cover
(astronaut floating in space/Johnathan Knowles), pp.16 (sea turtle/danilovi),
18 (rehabilitating sea turtle/Moment Open), 25 (boy using binoculars/
Joel Sartore), 34–35 (children reading map/Pauline St. Denis/Corbis/VCG),
39 (lighthouse in fog/olaser), 48–49 (woman and child signing/inhauscreative),
53 (man on laptop/JohnnyGreig), 76–77 (reef divers/ultramarinfoto);
Shutterstock: pp.6–7 (visitors at an aquarium/i-m-a-g-e), 8 (coral reef/Rich
Carey), 13 (diver filming sharks/VisionDive), 14 (manta ray/Konstantin
Novikov), 15 (photographing water droplets/Ray Bond), 20–21 (children on
ropes course/David Tadevosian), 28 (boy in winter clothing/Cozy nook), 29 (girl
in science lab/Joey Chung), 32 (kingfisher/Rudmer Zwerver), (photographer/
Iam_Anupong), 52 (young adults/Rawpixel.com), 62–63 (sporty children/
Mandy Godbehear), 74 (children playing soccer/Nieuwland Photography),
83 (scientists in Antarctica/Stu Shaw), 88 (Nellie Bly/Everett Historical)

Workbook

Illustrations by: EMC Design pp.95, 101, 103, 105, 113; Peter Francis/MB Artists
p.111; Anthony Lewis/MB Artists pp.99; Juan Moreno/MB Artists p.107; John
White/The Neis Group p.109

*The Publishers would like to thank the following for their kind permission to reproduce
photographs and other copyright material*: Oxford University Press: p.97 (inline
skates/Shutterstock), (electric guitar/Shutterstock); Shutterstock: pp.91 (girl at
water park/Rad K), 93 (manta ray/Konstantin Novikiv), 95 (boy on ropes course/
David Tadevosian)

Table of Contents

Hi! I'm Olly.

Hi, I'm Molly!

Introduction

Welcome to Oxford Skills World

Oxford Skills World: Reading with Writing is a flexible paired skills course that takes students on a journey toward independent learning, providing them with strategies and support to reach their goals.

For Students

- Student Book / Workbook
- Student's website with downloadable audio and extra resources
  www.oup.com/elt/oxfordskillsworld

For Teachers

- Downloadable Teacher's Pack with instructional support, assessment, professional development videos, projects, and writing resources
- Classroom Presentation Tool
- Teacher's website with downloadable audio and extra resources
  www.oup.com/elt/teacher/oxfordskillsworld

Be the Leader on Your Skills Adventure!

Hi! We're Olly and Molly, your skills adventure guides. We help you reach your goals by introducing new reading and writing strategies, asking helpful questions, and giving friendly reminders. Most importantly, we cheer you on every step of the way! Let's go!

Quick Guide

Inside Each Topic

Topic Opener

Theme-based topics provide high-interest content relevant to students' lives.

My Goals introduces students to the objectives of each unit in the topic.*

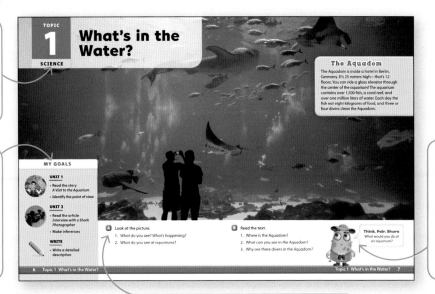

Fun characters, Olly and Molly, encourage 21st century skills like critical thinking, collaboration, and communication.

Students answer questions to activate prior knowledge and think critically.

Get Ready to Read • Read

Reading Goals are strategies students can apply to any text.

Before they read, students practice applying the unit's **Reading Goal** and identify new vocabulary.

Olly and Molly support students as they apply **Reading Goals** to each text.

At the end of each lesson, students assess the progress they are making toward achieving their goals.

*Each topic contains two thematically related units.

Quick Guide

Understand

Students increase their comprehension of the text by applying reading strategies to what they have read.

Students complete activities focused on reading comprehension and critical thinking.

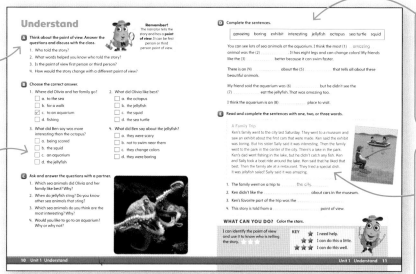

Vocabulary application activities strengthen students' comprehension of the unit's new language.

Additional texts and activities prepare students for task types found on standardized exams, such as Cambridge English: Young Learners.

Reading Check

With helpful reminders from Olly and Molly, students apply the **Reading Goals** from both units to a new text.

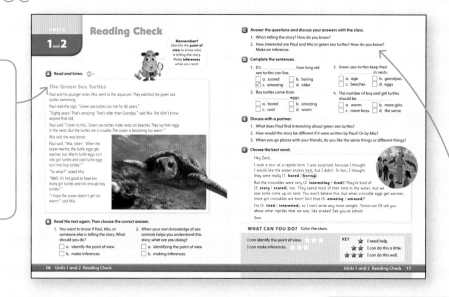

Students complete activities to boost comprehension and vocabulary application.

Get Ready to Write • Write

Writing Goals prepare students to write in different genres.

Writing Tips provide guidance on grammar, punctuation, and mechanics and help students write fluently and accurately.

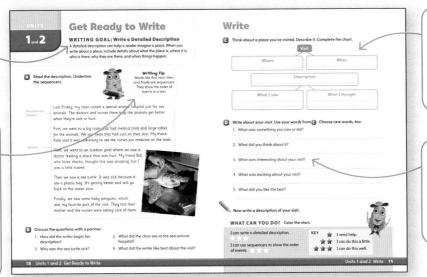

Students use graphic organizers to organize their thoughts for their own writing.

Thought-provoking questions help students generate ideas they will use in their own writing.

Workbook

Workbook pages at the end of the book provide more opportunities for students to apply their **Reading Goals** and boost comprehension.

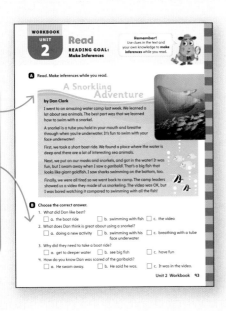

Additional activities provide extra opportunities for vocabulary comprehension and usage.

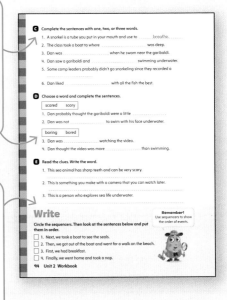

Students apply the topic's **Writing Tip** to ensure proper usage in their own writing.

What's in the Water?

MY GOALS

UNIT 1

- Read the story
  A Visit to the Aquarium
- Identify the point of view

UNIT 2

- Read the article
  Interview with a Shark Photographer
- Make inferences

WRITE

- Write a detailed description

 A Look at the picture.

1. What do you see? What's happening?
2. What do you see at aquariums?

The Aquadom

The Aquadom is inside a hotel in Berlin, Germany. It's 25 meters high—that's 12 floors. You can ride a glass elevator through the center of the aquarium! The aquarium contains over 1,500 fish, a coral reef, and over one million liters of water. Each day the fish eat eight kilograms of food, and three or four divers clean the Aquadom.

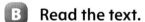 **B** **Read the text.**

1. Where is the Aquadom?

2. What can you see in the Aquadom?

3. Why are there divers in the Aquadom?

Think, Pair, Share
What would you do at an aquarium?

Read

READING GOAL: Identify the Point of View

A narrator tells the story and has a point of view. A first person point of view uses *I*, *me*, *we*, and *us* in the story. This narrator is a main character. A narrator with a third person point of view tells the story but is not part of the story.

Get Ready

A Read the sentences below. What is the point of view? Choose the correct answer.

1. Olivia doesn't like swimming.
   - ☐ a. first person
   - ☐ b. third person

2. We went to the museum with Emma and Lou on Saturday.
   - ☐ a. first person
   - ☐ b. third person

B Find the key words in the text. Look up the words you don't know in your dictionary.

C Read and listen to the story *A Visit to the Aquarium.* 🔊 2

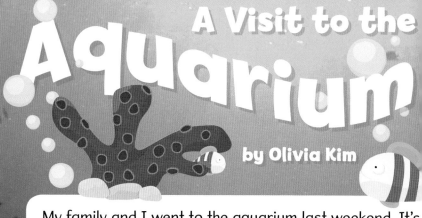

A Visit to the Aquarium
by Olivia Kim

My family and I went to the aquarium last weekend. It's a big aquarium and we walked around for hours. We sa[w] many different types of fish and other sea animals.

My dad liked the octopus the best. He said they're
5 interesting animals because they can change color to match their surroundings. I read that they're very smart animals, too. My brother Ben said the squid was more interesting than the octopus because it can swim faster. I agree with my dad, though. I think the octopus
10 is more interesting than the squid because of the way it changes colors.

I think I liked the special exhibit about jellyfish the best. Jellyfish are really amazing animals. They push water very fast out of their mouths. This is how they
15 move around!

Jellyfish eat fish and almost anything else they find, but not plants. They sting their food before eating it. They als[o] sting if they feel like they're in danger. So it's important not to swim near jellyfish, because they can sting if you
20 touch them.

Who is telling the story? Is it first person or third person **point of view**? Underline the words that show you.

In the aquarium, the jellyfish were peaceful to watch because they move slowly. Many jellyfish are clear, but others are beautiful colors, like pink and blue.

25 At first, Ben said the jellyfish were boring. But then a sea turtle swam by and ate one of the jellyfish! Ben really liked that. I felt sad for the jellyfish. I think my brother liked this part of our visit a lot more than I did.

WHAT CAN YOU DO? Color the stars.

I can read the story and identify the point of view. ★ ★ ★

I can understand all the key words. ★ ★ ★

KEY
★ I need help.
★ ★ I can do this a little.
★ ★ ★ I can do this well.

Understand

A Think about the point of view. Answer the questions and discuss with the class.

Remember!
The narrator tells the story and has a **point of view**. It can be first person or third person point of view.

1. Who told the story?

2. What words helped you know who told the story?

3. Is the point of view first person or third person?

4. How would the story change with a different point of view?

B Choose the correct answer.

1. Where did Olivia and her family go?
   - ☐ a. to the sea
   - ☐ b. for a walk
   - ☑ c. to an aquarium
   - ☐ d. fishing

2. What did Olivia like best?
   - ☐ a. the octopus
   - ☐ b. the jellyfish
   - ☐ c. the squid
   - ☐ d. the sea turtle

3. What did Ben say was more interesting than the octopus?
   - ☐ a. being scared
   - ☐ b. the squid
   - ☐ c. an aquarium
   - ☐ d. the jellyfish

4. What did Ben say about the jellyfish?
   - ☐ a. they were scary
   - ☐ b. not to swim near them
   - ☐ c. they change colors
   - ☐ d. they were boring

C Ask and answer the questions with a partner.

1. Which sea animals did Olivia and her family like best? Why?

2. When do jellyfish sting? Do you know other sea animals that sting?

3. Which sea animals do you think are the most interesting? Why?

4. Would you like to go to an aquarium? Why or why not?

Complete the sentences.

> amazing boring exhibit interesting jellyfish octopus sea turtle squid

You can see lots of sea animals at the aquarium. I think the most (1) ___amazing___ animal was the (2) _____. It has eight legs and can change colors! My friends like the (3) _____ better because it can swim faster.

There is an (4) _____ about the (5) _____ that tells all about these beautiful animals.

My friend said the aquarium was (6) _____ but he didn't see the (7) _____ eat the jellyfish. That was amazing too.

I think the aquarium is an (8) _____ place to visit.

E **Read and complete the sentences with one, two, or three words.**

A Family Trip

Ken's family went to the city last Saturday. They went to a museum and saw an exhibit about the first cars that were made. Ken said the exhibit was boring. But his sister Sally said it was interesting. Then the family went to the park in the center of the city. There's a lake in the park. Ken's dad went fishing in the lake, but he didn't catch any fish. Ken and Sally took a boat ride around the lake. Ken said that he liked that best. Then the family ate at a restaurant. They tried a special dish. It was jellyfish salad! Sally said it was amazing.

1. The family went on a trip to _____the city._____

2. Ken didn't like the _____ about cars in the museum.

3. Ken's favorite part of the trip was the _____

4. This story is told from a _____ point of view.

WHAT CAN YOU DO? Color the stars.

I can identify the point of view and use it to know who is telling the story. ★★★

KEY		
★	I need help.
★★	I can do this a little.
★★★	I can do this well.

Read

READING GOAL: Make Inferences

An inference is a guess about something the writer doesn't tell you in the text. You use clues in the text and your own knowledge to make an inference. Make inferences while you read to understand the story.

Get Ready

A Read the sentences below. Choose the correct inference.

1. The people in the audience were using their phones during the awards ceremony.

   ☐ a. They were interested.

   ☐ b. They were bored.

2. The man saw a shark swimming near him. He screamed.

   ☐ a. The man was tired.

   ☐ b. The man was scared.

B Find the key words in the text. Look up the words you don't know in your dictionary.

C Read and listen to the article *Interview with a Shark Photographer.* 🔊 3

Interview with a Shark Photographer

by Jack Lee

Nora Smith is a photographer. She is a diver and she takes pictures underwater. People really like her videos of sharks. We interviewed her for the school paper.

5 **Jack:** Nora, how did you become an underwater photographer?

Nora: Well, I was working as a photographer. And I started scuba diving. It's so beautiful underwater. There are so many different and colorful fish to see and I wanted to photograph them.

Jack: Was it difficult to go from taking photos on land to under the water?

Nora: Taking photos under the water is more difficult and more interesting. For one thing, there's less light and everything is moving. Once I learned how to take photos in those surroundings, I was bored taking photos on land. For me, taking photos on land isn't as interesting as taking photos underwater.

10

15

20

Jack: And how did you begin to take photos and record videos of sharks?

Nora: One day, I was diving and taking photos of some seals. Suddenly, a shark grabbed a seal and swam away! It happened very quickly. I was scared, but I kept taking photos.

25

After that, I started making videos. For me, seeing a shark isn't as scary as not taking a good photo of it!

Jack: Now, you travel a lot for work. Do you get tired?

30

Nora: Flying long distances on airplanes does make me tired, but I have too much fun making shark videos to let that stop me!

Does Nora like her job? How do you know? Make an **inference**.

WHAT CAN YOU DO? Color the stars.

I can read the article and use it to make inferences. ⭐⭐⭐

I can understand all the key words. ⭐⭐⭐

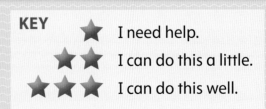

KEY
⭐ I need help.
⭐⭐ I can do this a little.
⭐⭐⭐ I can do this well.

Understand

A Think about making inferences. Answer the questions and discuss with the class.

1. What inferences can you make about Nora?
2. What clues helped you make those inferences?
3. How would you describe Nora?
4. Why is it important to make inferences when you read?

B Read. Choose **T** for **True** and **F** for **False**.

1. Nora combines diving with taking photos underwater.	T	F
2. Nora likes taking photos underwater because it's easy.	T	F
3. It's darker under the water than on land.	T	F
4. Nora saw a seal eat a shark one time.	T	F
5. Nora records videos of sharks because they eat seals.	T	F
6. Nora thinks making shark videos is fun.	T	F
7. Nora doesn't travel a lot for work.	T	F
8. Nora said flying on airplanes is scary.	T	F

C Ask and answer the questions with a partner.

1. How did Nora become an underwater photographer?
2. Why does Nora like to take photos underwater?
3. How do you think taking photos is different than recording videos?
4. What can you see underwater?
5. Do you think Nora likes to try new things? Why or why not?

D Choose the correct answer.

1. In line 1, *diver* means
   - [ ] a. swimming.
   - [ ] b. an underwater photographer.
   - [✔] c. a person who scuba dives.
   - [ ] d. a person who drives a boat.

2. Which words are the closest in meaning to *bored* in line 18?
   - [ ] a. not interested in
   - [ ] b. too tired to do something
   - [ ] c. finds too difficult
   - [ ] d. doing something many times

3. In line 24, what are *seals*?
   - [ ] a. a kind of shark
   - [ ] b. underwater plants
   - [ ] c. animals that live in the water
   - [ ] d. a kind of sea turtle

4. In line 28, *scary* means something that
   - [ ] a. you don't like to do.
   - [ ] b. makes you frightened.
   - [ ] c. you are doing for the first time.
   - [ ] d. you like to do.

E Read the text. Then read the questions and choose the correct answer.

Melanie,

Sorry you couldn't come to the museum today. There were some great photos. The photographer took them during a very rainy day. She made simple pictures of rain and puddles look really interesting.

It's going to rain tomorrow. Let's go out and take pictures. I want to try to take some amazing photos!

Erin

1. Why is Erin sorry Melanie didn't come to the museum? Because Melanie
   - [ ] a. didn't see the photos.
   - [ ] b. likes rain.
   - [ ] c. was not feeling well.
   - [ ] d. looked interesting.

2. How does Erin feel about taking photos in the rain?
   - [ ] a. scared
   - [ ] b. tired
   - [ ] c. bored
   - [ ] d. interested

WHAT CAN YOU DO? Color the stars.

I can make inferences and use them to understand a text.
⭐⭐⭐

KEY
⭐ I need help.
⭐⭐ I can do this a little.
⭐⭐⭐ I can do this well.

Reading Check

Remember!
Identify the **point of view** to know who is telling the story. Make **inferences** while you read.

A Read and listen. 🔊 4

The Green Sea Turtles

Paul and his younger sister, Mia, went to the aquarium. They watched the green sea turtles swimming.

Paul read the sign, "Green sea turtles can live for 80 years."

"Eighty years! That's amazing! That's older than Grandpa," said Mia. She didn't know anyone that old.

Paul said, "Listen to this. 'Green sea turtles make nests on beaches. They lay their eggs in the nests. But the turtles are in trouble. The ocean is becoming too warm.'"

Mia said she was bored.

Paul said, "Mia, listen! 'When the ocean warms, the turtle eggs get warmer, too. Warm turtle eggs turn into girl turtles and cool turtle eggs turn into boy turtles!'"

"So what?" asked Mia.

"Well, it's not good to have too many girl turtles and not enough boy turtles!'"

"I hope the ocean doesn't get too warm!" said Mia.

B Read the text again. Then choose the correct answer.

1. You want to know if Paul, Mia, or someone else is telling the story. What should you do?

   ☐ a. identify the point of view

   ☐ b. make inferences

2. When your own knowledge of sea animals helps you understand this story, what are you doing?

   ☐ a. identifying the point of view

   ☐ b. making inferences

C Answer the questions and discuss your answers with the class.

1. Who's telling the story? How do you know?

2. How interested are Paul and Mia in green sea turtles? How do you know? Make an inference.

D Complete the sentences.

1. It's _____ how long old sea turtles can live.
   - ☐ a. scared
   - ☐ b. boring
   - ☑ c. amazing
   - ☐ d. older

2. Green sea turtles keep their _____ in nests.
   - ☐ a. age
   - ☐ b. grandpas
   - ☐ c. beaches
   - ☐ d. eggs

3. Boy turtles come from _____ eggs.
   - ☐ a. bored
   - ☐ b. amazing
   - ☐ c. cool
   - ☐ d. warm

4. The number of boy and girl turtles should be _____
   - ☐ a. warm.
   - ☐ b. more girls.
   - ☐ c. more boys.
   - ☐ d. the same.

E Discuss with a partner.

1. What does Paul find interesting about green sea turtles?

2. How would the story be different if it were written by Paul? Or by Mia?

3. When you go places with your friends, do you like the same things or different things?

F Choose the best word.

Hey Zack,

I took a tour at a reptile farm. I was surprised, because I thought I would like the water snakes best, but I didn't. In fact, I thought they were really (1. **bored** / **boring**).

But the crocodiles were very (2. **interesting** / **tired**)! They're kind of (3. **scary** / **scared**), too. They spend most of their time in the water, but we saw some come up on land. You won't believe this, but when crocodile eggs get warmer, more girl crocodiles are born! Isn't that (4. **amazing** / **amazed**)?

I'm (5. **tired** / **interested**), so I can't write any more tonight. Tomorrow I'll tell you about other reptiles that we saw, like snakes! See you at school.

Sam

WHAT CAN YOU DO? Color the stars.

I can identify the point of view. ★ ★ ★

I can make inferences. ★ ★ ★

KEY

★ I need help.

★ ★ I can do this a little.

★ ★ ★ I can do this well.

Get Ready to Write

WRITING GOAL: Write a Detailed Description

A detailed description can help a reader imagine a place. When you write about a place, include details about what the place is, where it is, who is there, why they are there, and when things happen.

A Read the description. Underline the sequencers.

> **Writing Tip**
> Words like *first*, *next*, *then*, and *finally* are sequencers. They show the order of events in a text.

Introduction of place

Last Friday, my class visited a special animal hospital just for sea animals. The doctors and nurses there help the animals get better when they're sick or hurt.

Details

First, we went to <u>a big room that had medical tools and large tables</u> for the animals. <u>We saw seals that had cuts on their skin</u>. My friend Kate said it was interesting to see the nurses put medicine on the seals.

Next, <u>we went to an outdoor pool where we saw a doctor feeding a shark</u> that was hurt. My friend Bill, who loves sharks, thought this was amazing, but I was a little scared.

Then we saw a sea turtle. It was sick because it ate a plastic bag. It's getting better and will go back to the ocean soon.

Finally, we saw some baby penguins, which was my favorite part of the visit. They lost their mother and the nurses were taking care of them.

B Discuss the questions with a partner.

1. How did the writer begin her description?

2. What did the class see at the sea animal hospital?

3. Why was the sea turtle sick?

4. What did the writer like best about the visit?

Write

C Think about a place you've visited. Describe it. Complete the chart.

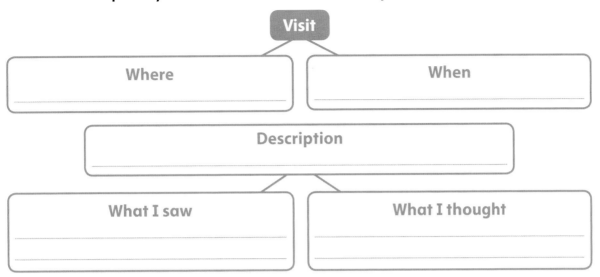

D Write about your visit. Use your words from C. Choose new words, too.

1. What was something you saw or did?

   _____

2. What did you think about it?

   _____

3. What was interesting about your visit?

   _____

4. What was exciting about your visit?

   _____

5. What did you like the best?

   _____

   Now write a description of your visit.

WHAT CAN YOU DO?   Color the stars.

I can write a detailed description.
⭐⭐⭐

I can use sequencers to show the order
of events. ⭐⭐⭐

KEY
⭐ I need help.
⭐⭐ I can do this a little.
⭐⭐⭐ I can do this well.

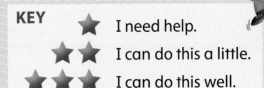

TOPIC 2

HEALTH

What to Wear

MY GOALS

UNIT 3

- Read the newsletter *Field Day*
- Identify the main idea and details

UNIT 4

- Read the story *Who Was That?*
- Identify the main idea and theme

WRITE

- Write a magazine article

 A Look at the picture.

1. What do you see? What are the people doing?

2. What are the people wearing? Why do you think they are dressed that way?

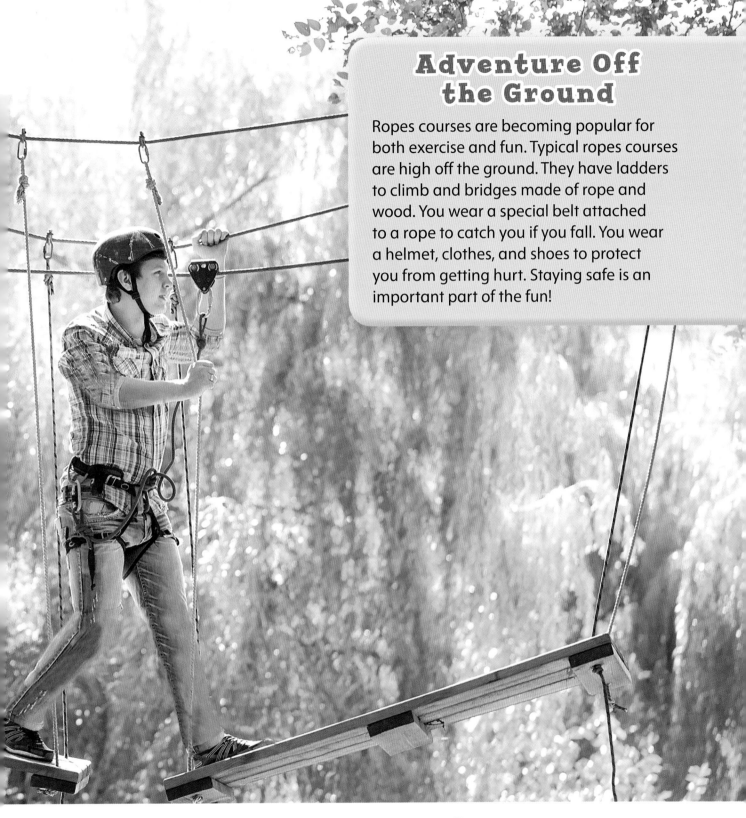

Adventure Off the Ground

Ropes courses are becoming popular for both exercise and fun. Typical ropes courses are high off the ground. They have ladders to climb and bridges made of rope and wood. You wear a special belt attached to a rope to catch you if you fall. You wear a helmet, clothes, and shoes to protect you from getting hurt. Staying safe is an important part of the fun!

B Read the text.

1. Why do people do a ropes course?

2. Why do you need to wear a helmet on a ropes course?

3. Have you ever tried to do something like a ropes course? What was it like?

Think, Pair, Share
What kinds of things do you wear for safety? When do you wear them?

Read

READING GOAL: Identify the Main Idea and Details

Each paragraph in a text has a main idea and details. Details explain why the main idea is true. When you read, find the main idea of each paragraph. Then find the details to learn more about each main idea.

Get Ready

A **Read the paragraph below. Choose the correct answer.**

Safety is important. A hat protects you from sunburn. A helmet protects your head if you fall.

1. What is the main idea?
   - [ ] a. A helmet protects your head.
   - [ ] b. Safety is important.

2. What is a detail?
   - [ ] a. A helmet protects your head.
   - [ ] b. Safety is important.

B **Find the key words in the text. Look up words you don't know in your dictionary.**

C **Read and listen to the newsletter *Field Day*.** 🔊 5

Dear Students,

Are you ready for Field Day? Now that the weather is warm, it's time to turn off the TV and go outside! We're going to have a lot of fun
5 outdoor activities to do.

Make sure you get up extra early because the Birding Competition starts at exactly 7 a.m.! You'll work in teams of three or four to create a list of different kinds of birds that live in the
10 park. Teams may watch birds throughout the day, but remember that birds are most active in the early morning.

The main event will be the ropes course, which includes ladders and bridges. You *must* wear
15 a helmet for this event because you'll be high off the ground. Your head must be protected in case of a fall, so please bring a helmet if you own one.

If the weather is warm, we'll go canoeing! You
20 *must* wear a life jacket in the canoes, even if you're a good swimmer. I was in a canoe last year and I accidentally fell out of the boat, so you should take off your watch and leave your cell phone on dry land. (Mine both got wet and
25 I had to get new ones!)

A teacher will be handing out a scarf to each student. Teams will receive matching scarves. Wearing one around your neck also provides extra sun protection. Be sure to put on sunscreen, and
30 I strongly recommend wearing a wide hat.

Come prepared for lots of Field Day fun in the sun!

Ms. Lee

What is the **main idea** of the third paragraph? What **details** support it? Underline the words that tell you.

WHAT CAN YOU DO?   Color the stars.

I can read the newsletter and find the main ideas and details.   ★ ★ ★

I can understand all the key words.   ★ ★ ★

KEY

★ I need help.

★ ★ I can do this a little.

★ ★ ★ I can do this well.

Understand

Remember!
Each paragraph has a **main idea**. **Details** help you understand the main idea.

A Think about the main ideas and details. Answer the questions and discuss with the class.

1. What is the main idea of the first paragraph?

2. Why should students make sure they get up early for Field Day?

3. What do you have to wear if you go canoeing?

4. What are the scarves for?

B Choose the correct answer.

1. When should students start watching birds?

   ☐ a. before they put on sunscreen
   ☐ b. early in the morning
   ☐ c. while they go canoeing
   ☐ d. after climbing the ropes course

2. What must students wear on the ropes course?

   ☐ a. a watch
   ☐ b. a scarf
   ☐ c. a life jacket
   ☐ d. a helmet

3. For which activity should students take off their watches?

   ☐ a. wearing a helmet
   ☐ b. bird watching
   ☐ c. rope climbing
   ☐ d. canoeing

4. What happened to Ms. Lee at last year's Field Day?

   ☐ a. She got a sunburn.
   ☐ b. She lost her watch.
   ☐ c. She fell out of the boat.
   ☐ d. She wore a helmet.

C Ask and answer the questions with a partner.

1. What activities do you wear a helmet for? Why do you wear one?

2. What do you do to stay safe in the sun?

3. Would you like to try a ropes course? Why or why not?

4. Have you ever been canoeing? Did you like it? Why or why not?

D Complete the sentences.

> competition   helmet   life jackets   scarf   sunscreen
>
> take off my watch   turned off the TV   watch birds

Field Day was so much fun! I forgot to put on (1) _____, but luckily, Ms. Lee had extra. I had my bike (2) _____ to wear on the ropes course. Everyone put on (3) _____ when we went canoeing. We were about to get into the water when I remembered to (4) _____.

A counselor gave everyone on my team a purple (5) _____ to wear around our necks. We didn't start to (6) _____ until 8 a.m. My team had the longest list so we won the birding (7) _____! The prize was a T-shirt with beautiful pictures of birds.

I was too tired to do anything when I got home. I (8) _____ and went to bed.

E Read and complete the sentences with one, two, or three words.

My New Hobby by Leo Mura

My favorite hobby is called *birding*. I always learn something new when I watch birds—they're very interesting! There are many birding competitions, like the World Series of Birding.

Before I go to bed, I pick out the clothes I'll need the next morning. On sunny days, I put on sunscreen, a hat, and a long-sleeved shirt for sun protection. On rainy days, I wear rubber boots to protect my feet from mud. In the morning, I eat breakfast quickly, get dressed, and go looking for birds!

1. The main idea of the first paragraph is Leo's _____

2. Leo thinks birds are very _____

3. The World Series of Birding is a _____

4. On sunny days, Leo puts on sunscreen, a _____, and a _____

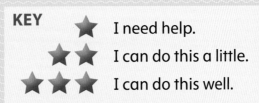

WHAT CAN YOU DO? Color the stars.

I can use the main ideas and details to understand a text. ★ ★ ★

KEY
★ I need help.
★ ★ I can do this a little.
★ ★ ★ I can do this well.

Read

READING GOAL: Identify the Main Idea and Theme

The main idea is what a story is about. The theme is a lesson you can learn from the story. After you read, ask, *What is this story about?* to find the main idea. Then ask, *What did I learn?* to find the theme.

Get Ready

A Read the paragraph below. Then write **M** for the main idea and **T** for the theme.

Reza slept late yesterday. He got on his bike, but forgot to put on a helmet. He was in a hurry, crashed into a tree, and hurt his head!

1. Reza had an accident. _____

2. You should always wear a helmet when you ride a bike. _____

B Find the key words in the text. Look up words you don't know in your dictionary.

C Read and listen to the story *Who Was That?* 🔊 6

Who Was That?

by Johan Jonasson

Last winter I acted in a play at school. I read a lot of books, so we used one of my favorite stories to write the play. It was about two boys who looked so much alike, no one could tell them apart!

5　One cold day we turned in our homework and stayed after school to work on costumes. We threw our jackets, hats, and things in a pile, turned up the heat, and turned on some music.

Where I live, you need a lot of clothes to protect you
10　from the cold, so you might not see your neighbor's face all winter! You recognize people by their clothes instead of their faces. All of my friends know me because I wear a bright blue coat.

My character in the play needed glasses and a belt
15　to carry tools. Eva said she had the perfect belt at home. It was cold outside, so she needed a jacket, but hers was buried in the pile. She borrowed my jacket and some mittens to cover her hands.

20 Just after Eva left, our teacher came into the room. He asked us to turn down the music, because it was pretty loud. Then he said, "I just turned off the computer when I saw Johan leaving, but …" He looked confused when he saw me there. "Johan?"

"You saw Eva," I said. "She was wearing my blue coat."

25 My teacher laughed. "I should have looked closer," he said. "I can't believe I got confused because of your coat."

I said, "That's OK. Two kids looking alike is just what our play is about!"

What is the **main idea** of the story? What is the **theme**? Underline the main idea and circle the words that show the theme.

WHAT CAN YOU DO? Color the stars.

I can read the story and identify the main idea and theme. ★ ★ ★

I can understand all the key words. ★ ★ ★

KEY
★ I need help.
★ ★ I can do this a little.
★ ★ ★ I can do this well.

Understand

Remember!
The **main idea** is what a story is about. The **theme** is what you can learn from a story.

A Think about finding a theme and main idea. Answer the questions and discuss with the class.

1. What is the story about?

2. What mistake did the teacher make?

3. What can you learn from the teacher's mistake?

B Read. Choose **T** for **True** and **F** for **False**.

1. Johan reads a lot of books.	T	F
2. Mittens are worn on the feet.	T	F
3. Eva owns a bright-blue jacket.	T	F
4. The story takes place on a cold day.	T	F
5. We need clothes to protect us from cold weather.	T	F
6. Eva went home to get a belt.	T	F
7. Eva borrowed a jacket to fool her teacher.	T	F
8. The teacher recognized Eva when she left.	T	F

C Ask and answer the questions with a partner.

1. What are the seasons like where you live?

2. What special clothes do you have for different seasons?

3. Who can you recognize by the clothes they wear? What do they wear?

4. Have you ever acted in a play? If you have, what was the play about? If you haven't, do you think you would like to act in a play? Why or why not?

5. What kinds of activities do you do after school?

D Choose the correct answer.

1. In line 7, *turned up* means to
   - ☐ a. create.
   - ☐ b. end.
   - ☐ c. raise.
   - ☐ d. need.

2. In line 14, *belt* means something that
   - ☐ a. helps you see.
   - ☐ b. holds your tools.
   - ☐ c. looks like you.
   - ☐ d. keeps you warm.

3. In line 20, *turn down* means
   - ☐ a. feel happy.
   - ☐ b. is confused.
   - ☐ c. look closely.
   - ☐ d. make less noise.

4. In line 21, *turned off* means
   - ☐ a. sent a message online.
   - ☐ b. protected from the cold.
   - ☐ c. stopped the power.
   - ☐ d. recognized friends.

E Read the text. Then read the questions and choose the correct answer.

Safe Science

Allie is learning about science class safety. In a science lab, you may work with fire and ice, so you need to protect yourself. Before you turn up the heat, be sure you are wearing the right things!

Everyone must wear safety glasses at all times in a lab. They protect your eyes from heat, splashes, and spills. Wear closed shoes and a lab coat to protect your skin and clothes. To keep your hands safe, take off your watch and any jewelry, so they don't get caught on equipment. Put on gloves to protect your hands. Once you're covered, you can relax and focus on science!

1. What do you need to do before starting science lab?
   - ☐ a. put on the right clothes
   - ☐ b. watch out for spills
   - ☐ c. turn up the heat
   - ☐ d. relax and focus

2. What do shoes, gloves, safety glasses, and a lab coat do?
   - ☐ a. make materials hot or cold
   - ☐ b. protect your skin and eyes
   - ☐ c. get caught on equipment
   - ☐ d. hold liquids and other materials

WHAT CAN YOU DO? Color the stars.

I can identify the main idea and the theme of a story. ★★★

KEY
★ I need help.
★★ I can do this a little.
★★★ I can do this well.

Reading Check

Remember!
Identify the **main idea**, **details**, and **theme** to know more about the story.

A Read and listen. 🔊 7

Help Needed!

Yesterday's storm left lots of small tree branches and trash along Arrow Avenue. Please join us on Saturday morning to help clean up! We'll start at 9 a.m. by the library and we need all the help we can get!

Please wear light-colored clothes. Alice will hand out bright orange vests. The clothes and vests help make everyone easy to see, so drivers will know to be extra careful where we're working.

Make sure to put on sunscreen, and bring work gloves to protect your hands. We'll need some people to cut loose branches from trees, so if you have a helmet, please bring it with you.

Please bring as many people as you can. We have a lot of work to do, but the more helpers we have, the easier it will be!

ARROW AVE

B Read the text again. Then choose the correct answer.

1. You want to know what kind of clothes to wear. What should you do?

   ☐ a. identify the main idea

   ☐ b. identify the details

2. When you read the text, you learned that working with others is helpful. What did you do?

   ☐ a. identified the main idea

   ☐ b. identified the theme

C Answer the questions and discuss your answers with the class.

1. What's the main idea of each paragraph?

2. What details in the text are about safety? How do you know?

D Complete the sentences.

1. A _____ made a big mess.

☐ a. bag ☐ b. glove

☐ c. storm ☐ d. vest

2. Alice will hand out _____

☐ a. branches. ☐ b. clothes.

☐ c. safety glasses. ☐ d. vests.

3. People should bring a _____ if they will be cutting branches.

☐ a. gloves ☐ b. helmet

☐ c. sunscreen ☐ d. vests

4. The helpers should wear _____ to protect them from the sun.

☐ a. gloves ☐ b. sunscreen

☐ c. a vest ☐ d. a helmet

E Discuss with a partner.

1. What event does this flyer describe?

2. Why would some of the helpers need to wear helmets?

3. Why should helpers be easy to see?

F Choose the best word.

I go to the beach every weekend with friends. I wear a (1. **helmet / life jacket**) because we ride our bikes there. There's a special bike path, so we can ride pretty fast. It's always a (2. **competition / watch**) to see who gets there first!

One of my favorite things to do at the beach is to read a lot of (3. **books / scarves**). I got a terrible sunburn once, so I always wear (4. **mittens / sunscreen**) now. Sometimes I take a (5. **hat / vest**) for more sun protection. At the end of the day, I sometimes get cold. I have a special (6. **scarf / vest**) just for this!

WHAT CAN YOU DO? Color the stars.

I can find the main idea and details of a paragraph. ⭐⭐⭐

I can find the main idea and theme for a text. ⭐⭐⭐

KEY

⭐ I need help.

⭐⭐ I can do this a little.

⭐⭐⭐ I can do this well.

Get Ready to Write

WRITING GOAL: Write a Magazine Article

A magazine article informs a reader about a topic. It includes a headline, pictures, and an interesting opening sentence that grabs the reader's attention. This sentence is called a *hook*.

A Read the magazine article.

Writing Tip
Capitalize the important words in a headline. Always capitalize the first and last words.

Headline

Watching Birds for Fun!

Hook — Have you ever wanted to learn about our great feather-covered friends? If so, become a birder! You'll find that every bird has its own story to tell. Birders are people who make a hobby of watching birds and some even enter friendly competitions.

You don't need much equipment for bird watching. But you will need clothes to protect you from nature and the weather. Hats, shirts with long sleeves, pants, and sunglasses are all good choices. And you want to stay hidden, so don't wear bright colors. Leave that favorite bright yellow scarf at home!

Pictures

There's a lot of information about birding. You may want to read a lot of books to learn where to find your favorite birds. Many birders are good photographers, so you might want to get a good camera.

B Discuss the questions with a partner.

1. How did the writer begin the article?

2. What do the words *feather-covered friends* refer to?

3. Why do birders need to stay hidden?

4. Do the pictures make you want to read the article? Why?

Write

C Think about an outdoor activity you enjoy. Complete the chart.

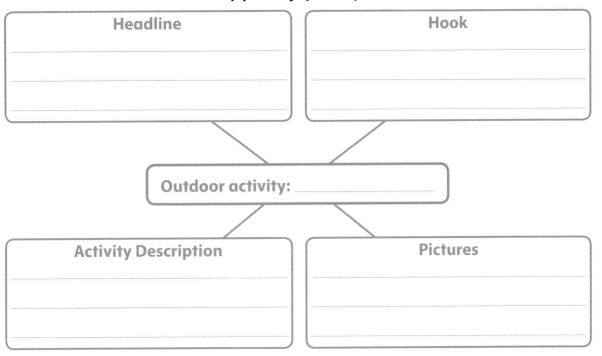

D Write about your activity. Use your words from **C**. Choose new words, too.

1. What is the outdoor activity you enjoy?

2. What is the headline for your article?

3. What is the hook?

4. How would you describe this activity? What pictures will you use?

Now write a magazine article about your outdoor activity.

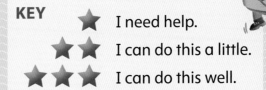

WHAT CAN YOU DO?   Color the stars.

I can write a headline and a hook.
⭐⭐⭐

I can write a magazine article. ⭐⭐⭐

KEY   ⭐ I need help.
⭐⭐ I can do this a little.
⭐⭐⭐ I can do this well.

MY GOALS

UNIT 5

- Read the story *Lost and Found*
- Identify and analyze the setting

UNIT 6

- Read the article *The World of Orienteering*
- Use visuals

WRITE

- Write a process essay

A Look at the picture.

1. What do you see in the picture? Where are the children?

2. What do you think they're doing? Why?

The Mighty Compass

The first compasses were used about eight hundred years ago. A compass is an instrument you use to tell direction. It has a small, pointed magnet that always points north. If you know where north is, you can always find south, west, and east. Use a compass with a map, and you can find your way anywhere!

B **Read the text.**

1. What is a compass?

2. How can you use a compass if you get lost?

3. Have you ever used a map? Where?

Think, Pair, Share
Have you used a compass with a map? Where were you?

Read

READING GOAL: Identify and Analyze the Setting

The setting is where and when a story happens. It can affect a story's characters and events. While you read, think about the setting. Ask yourself, *How does the writer describe it? How does it affect the characters and plot?*

Get Ready

A Read the sentences below. What is the setting? Choose the correct answer.

1. Len got water in his nose as he played in the waves.

   ☐ a. He's at the beach.

   ☐ b. He's in the city.

2. Emma asked the server for a glass of water.

   ☐ a. She's in a restaurant.

   ☐ b. She's in her kitchen at home.

B Find the key words in the text. Look up words you don't know in your dictionary.

C Read and listen to the story *Lost and Found.*
🔊 8

Lost and Found

Jaya and her family went hiking one foggy morning. Their goal was a hill with a tall, crooked tree on top. They liked to picnic there.

"I think we missed our turn," said Jaya. She pointed to a
5   log bench on the left side of the trail.

"Yeah, I don't remember this bench. There's a place we should have turned right, but I think we went straight," said her brother, Manoj.

Their mom looked at her watch, and added, "And
10   it's noon. We should be there by now."

They stopped and looked around at the trees. Jaya realized they were next to a different, smaller hill. She said, "Before we go back down the trail, we should hike up the hill and take a look around!"

15   "I'm tired," said Manoj. "I don't want to climb an extra hill."

"Why not? Let's go!" said their mom. So they walked up, and they discovered the top of the hill was above the fog. "Nice!" Mom said. "We know how to read a map, so let's look. There's the lighthouse near town. We know that's south, and I think we're on
20 a hill between the lighthouse and our usual picnic spot."

They looked at the map. Then they looked around and saw the top of another hill to the northeast. It had a tall, crooked tree on top.

"There it is!" said Jaya. "It looks like an island in a sea of clouds."

What is the **setting** of the story? Underline the words that tell you.

WHAT CAN YOU DO? Color the stars.

I can read the story and identify the setting.

⭐⭐⭐

I can understand all the key words. ⭐⭐⭐

KEY ⭐ I need help.

⭐⭐ I can do this a little.

⭐⭐⭐ I can do this well.

Understand

A Think about the setting. Answer the questions and discuss with the class.

Remember!
The **setting** is where and when the story happens. It affects the characters and events.

1. Where is the family in the story? What is the weather like?

2. How do Jaya and Manoj know they're in the wrong place?

3. What time of day is it when Jaya and her family see the bench?

4. How does weather affect the family's plans?

B Choose the correct answer.

1. What does the family do on the hill?
   - ☐ a. sit down
   - ☐ b. turn left
   - ☐ c. read a map
   - ☐ d. have a picnic

2. Where is the fog?
   - ☐ a. at the bottom of the hill
   - ☐ b. above the hill
   - ☐ c. to the north
   - ☐ d. off the main trail

3. How did Jaya and her family get on the wrong trail?
   - ☐ a. They went left.
   - ☐ b. They went straight.
   - ☐ c. They went up a hill.
   - ☐ d. They went back.

4. Where did Jaya and her family plan to hike to?
   - ☐ a. the bench
   - ☐ b. the lighthouse
   - ☐ c. the hill above the fallen log
   - ☐ d. the hill with the crooked tree

C Ask and answer the questions with a partner.

1. Have you ever gotten lost? How did you find your way back?

2. Has weather ever changed your plans? How?

3. Do you enjoy hiking? Why or why not?

4. Do you enjoy other outdoor activities? Which ones?

D Complete the sentences.

| between | go back | go straight | next to |
| on the left | read a map | turn right | up the hill |

My mom, my sister, and I went hiking in our favorite park last weekend. We usually
(1) _____ at a place where the main trail splits. On this trip,
we decided to (2) _____ instead of turning.

We knew where we were going, so we didn't need to (3) _____. Our plan
was to (4) _____ to an old, giant tree we once found by accident.

We walked until we saw a bench (5) _____ side of the trail, near a tall hill.
We were going to hike (6) _____, but it was a long climb, so we rested.

I sat down (7) _____ my sister on the bench. Mom sat down
(8) _____ us. But after only one minute, she asked, "Are you ready to hike?"

E Read and complete the sentences with one, two, or three words.

Warning! Warning!

A lighthouse is a tall tower built on the coast. The top of a lighthouse has
a huge lamp and a very loud horn. The light from the lamp can be seen
far out on the ocean. The horn can be heard far away. When fog forms,
someone goes to the lighthouse and turns on the light and horn. This warns
people in ships where the land is, telling them which direction *not* to go.

1. A lighthouse is a tall _____ built on the coast.

2. It has a bright _____ and very loud _____

3. These are turned on when _____ forms along the coast.

4. A lighthouse warns _____ that they are near land.

WHAT CAN YOU DO? Color the stars.

I can identify and analyze
the setting of a story. ★ ★ ★

KEY   ★ I need help.
      ★ ★ I can do this a little.
    ★ ★ ★ I can do this well.

Read

READING GOAL: Use Visuals

Pictures, diagrams, and maps are visuals. Visuals provide information that is not in a text. While you read, look at visuals to understand more about the ideas in a text.

Get Ready

A Read the sentences below. Choose the correct answer.

1. A visual gives the same information that is in a text.
   - ☐ a. true
   - ☐ b. false

2. A picture is an example of a visual.
   - ☐ a. true
   - ☐ b. false

B Find the key words in the text. Look up words you don't know in your dictionary.

C Read and listen to the article *The World of Orienteering*. 🔊 9

The World of Orienteering

Imagine you are in a new city. Standing on a corner, you ask someone how to get to a store. They tell you to "go two blocks north, turn left, and you'll be across the street from
5   the bookstore." Now imagine you are in an outdoor race. Instead of directions, you have only a map and a compass, and instead of running down a marked road, you run around in the woods. Welcome to orienteering!

10 In the sport of orienteering, racers use a map and compass to find stations, which are called controls. A special flag marks each control (see Figure 1). Controls are placed
15 so you can't see them easily from all directions. They may be in front of a big
20 rock or behind a tree, which means racers *must* use their maps and compasses to
25 find controls.

Figure 1

Orienteering Control Card					
Name					
Course	Age	Class	Start	Minutes	Seconds
			Finish	Minutes	Seconds
1	2	3	4	5	6
7	8	9	10	11	12
13	14	15	16	17	18

Figure 2

At each control, racers mark a card they carry with them (see Figure 2). The cards are very important because racers must find all the controls to win. If someone misses a control, they won't have that mark on their card. They might cross the finish line first, but the next person to finish with a full card will win the race.

In a race in a city, you might only need to cross the street to get to the finish line. In orienteering, you will likely run along a river, climb over rocks, and go up and down hills. And, after all that, you still have to use your compass to find the finish line!

How do the **visuals** help you understand the text?

WHAT CAN YOU DO?   Color the stars.

I can read the text and use visuals.   ★★★

I can understand all the key words.   ★★★

KEY   ★ I need help.

★★ I can do this a little.

★★★ I can do this well.

Understand

A Think about the visuals that go with the story. Answer the questions and discuss with the class.

1. How many visuals are there? What do they show?
2. What does a control flag look like?
3. Look at the card. How many controls are there?
4. How do visuals help you to understand a text?

B Read. Choose **T** for **True** and **F** for **False**.

1. Orienteering events are held outdoors.   T   F
2. In orienteering, you may only use a compass.   T   F
3. Control flags have bright colors.   T   F
4. Control flags are easy to find.   T   F
5. Racers carry cards that they mark.   T   F
6. Racers must know how to read a map.   T   F
7. Racers need a map and compass to find the finish line. T   F
8. You must finish first to win an orienteering event.   T   F

C Ask and answer the questions with a partner.

1. What outdoor sports have you tried?
2. What time of year do you think orienteering events are held? Why?
3. Is it important for orienteering racers to keep their cards? Why?
4. Do you think orienteering racers have to be good runners? Why?
5. Do you want to try orienteering? Why or why not?

D Choose the correct answer.

1. In line 2, *corner* means
   - ☐ a. a flag.
   - ☐ b. an event.
   - ☐ c. a place where two roads meet.
   - ☐ d. a spot behind a tree or rock.

2. In line 3, *Go two blocks* means
   - ☐ a. move this far.
   - ☐ b. hide over there.
   - ☐ c. turn around here.
   - ☐ d. run more quickly.

3. In line 4, *across the street from* means
   - ☐ a. behind.
   - ☐ b. in front.
   - ☐ c. on the other side.
   - ☐ d. next to.

4. In line 33, *cross the street* means
   - ☐ a. go to the other side.
   - ☐ b. climb over.
   - ☐ c. go up and down.
   - ☐ d. run around.

E Read the text. Then read the questions and choose the correct answer.

Treasure Hunt

My friend Bayani had the best party this weekend! He lives across the street from the park, and his family made a treasure hunt for us to do there. They gave us maps, compasses, and directions. My team's first direction said, "Start at the north corner of the swings. Then walk east for 50 steps." We were the first group to find a treasure! We ate them before we got back to Bayani's house.

1. Where is Bayani's house?
   - ☐ a. near a corner
   - ☐ b. north of the street
   - ☐ c. east of the swings
   - ☐ d. across from the park

2. What treasure did the writer's team find?
   - ☐ a. cookies
   - ☐ b. directions
   - ☐ c. maps
   - ☐ d. swings

WHAT CAN YOU DO? Color the stars.

I can use visuals to help me understand a text. ★★★

KEY
- ★ I need help.
- ★★ I can do this a little.
- ★★★ I can do this well.

Reading Check

Remember!
Identify the **setting** by asking yourself, *How does the writer describe it?* While you read, use **visuals** to help you understand the text.

A **Read and listen.** 🔊 10

Land, Ho!

A captain and two sailors were guiding their ship through rough water. The sun was shining, but clouds were moving quickly toward them. Suddenly, Susie yelled to the captain.

"Ahoy, Captain Laila! I see land at last!"

"Where?" cried the captain.

"Turn right a little," said Susie. "We need to go north!" The captain turned the ship's wheel.

"Hurry, the clouds are quickly moving in behind us," Marco called from the back of the ship. "Seriously, you guys, it's about to rain."

Again the captain spun the wheel, going back and forth across the rough sea. Suddenly she yelled, "We're there! Everyone swim for shore!"

At that moment, the first drops of rain fell. Everyone jumped from the ship and ran home.

B **Read the text again. Then choose the correct answer.**

1. Think about the words *ship*, *sun was shining*, and *about to rain* in the story. What do these words help you do?

   ☐ a. use visuals

   ☐ b. identify and analyze the setting

2. The sand, grass, and trees in the picture tell us that the characters are in a park, not in the ocean. What is this an example of?

   ☐ a. using visuals

   ☐ b. identifying and analyzing the setting

C Answer the questions and discuss your answers with the class.

1. What is the setting for the story?

2. How does the picture help you understand the story?

D Complete the sentences.

1. The *rough water* is probably _____ on the playground.

   ☐ a. children   ☐ b. ocean

   ☐ c. rain   ☐ d. sand

2. Susie tells Laila to _____

   ☐ a. hurry up.   ☐ b. jump off.

   ☐ c. look back.   ☐ d. turn right.

3. Marco is _____ of the ship.

   ☐ a. at the back   ☐ b. in the middle

   ☐ c. near the front   ☐ d. on the right side

4. Everyone went _____ because it was beginning to rain.

   ☐ a. behind   ☐ b. home

   ☐ c. out   ☐ d. right

E Discuss with a partner.

1. Who are the sailors in the story? How do you know?

2. What do the pretend and real settings of the story have in common?

3. Have you ever made up stories like this with friends?

F Choose the best word.

Susie, Laila, and Marco had to (1. **read a map / hurry**) to get home. They got to Susie's house first. Marco's house was (2. **across the street / above**) from hers, and Laila lived just (3. **up the hill / between**).

Luckily, the park was on a (4. **left / corner**) near all of their houses. They made plans to (5. **go back / turn left**) to the ship the next day, if it was sunny.

WHAT CAN YOU DO?   Color the stars.

I can identify and analyze the setting.   ★ ★ ★

I can use visuals.   ★ ★ ★

KEY

★   I need help.

★ ★   I can do this a little.

★ ★ ★   I can do this well.

Get Ready to Write

WRITING GOAL: Write a Process Essay

A process essay tells the reader how to do something. It has a title that explains what the reader will learn how to do. Each paragraph explains a step in the process.

A Read the essay. Underline the phrases that show the purpose of an instruction.

Writing Tip
Use phrases like *so that* and *in order to* to show the purpose of an instruction.

Title

How to Find the North Star at Night

The North Star is found in the sky above the North Pole, so it always lines up with north on a map. It's not a bright star. In order to find it, look for the group of stars called the Big Dipper. It looks like a square cup with a handle on the left.

Paragraphs that explain steps in the process

Find the star in the lower right corner of the Big Dipper's "bowl" (see *a* in the diagram). Imagine drawing a line between this star and the one above it (see *b* in the diagram).

Now imagine making this line longer so that it becomes an arrow pointing up. It will point to the North Star, which is also the star at the end of the "handle" in the Little Dipper. The Little Dipper is a smaller group of stars found just "above" the Big Dipper.

Now you can find the North Star at night!

B Discuss the questions with a partner.

1. What is special about the North Star?

2. Where is the Little Dipper compared to the Big Dipper?

3. How many steps are there to finding the North Star?

4. How does finding the Big Dipper help you find the North Star?

Write

C Think about a process you use often. Fill in the chart.

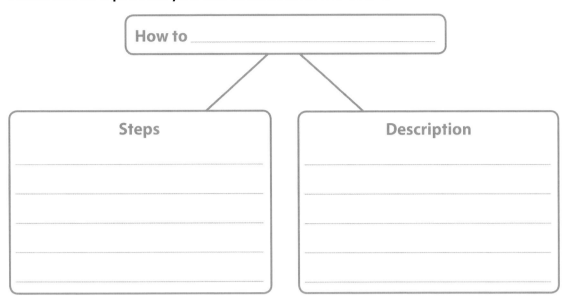

How to _____

Steps	Description

D Write about your process. Use your words from **C**. Choose new words, too.

1. What process do you want to explain?

    _____

2. What is the first step in the process?

    _____

3. What is the second step?

    _____

4. What is the last step?

    _____

Now write your process essay.

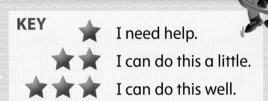

A World of Words

MY GOALS

UNIT 7

- Read the article *Languages We Use*
- Understand a bar graph

UNIT 8

- Read the story *So Many Questions*
- Make predictions

WRITE

- Write a review

A Look at the picture.

1. What are the people doing with their hands? Why?

2. Do you see people doing this in other places? Where?

How We Talk

There are many languages around the world. People who can't hear or speak use special languages called *sign languages*.

In sign languages, people "talk" using their hands to make signals. They also communicate by making different faces and moving their bodies. In American sign language, for instance, you can say "thank you" by putting your fingers on your chin and moving your hand out. This is also the sign for "you're welcome."

B Read the text.

1. How do you use language in school?

2. How does learning a language help you?

3. Would you like to learn a sign language? Why?

Think, Pair, Share
Where can you go to hear different languages?

READING GOAL: Understand a Bar Graph

A bar graph compares two or more things. It uses rectangles to show how much or how many. While you read, look at bar graphs to learn specific information that is not in the text.

Get Ready

A Look at the bar graph below. Choose the correct answer.

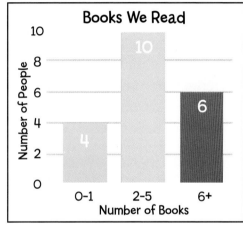

Books We Read

1. What does the ▮ bar show?

   ☐ a. how many students read no books or one book

   ☐ b. how many students read between two and five books

2. How many students read more than 6 books?

   ☐ a. 6   ☐ b. 10

B Find the key words in the text. Look up words you don't know in your dictionary.

C Read and listen to the article *Languages We Use*. ◄)) 11

Languages We Use

Everyone is a native speaker of their first language. This is the language you learned and speak at home. An official language is the one used by the government of a country. Most
5   people learn this in school. A country has to pass a law to make a language official.

Some countries have no official language. Mexico is one example. Most people there speak Spanish. Many Mexican people speak native languages,
10   too. But Mexico never passed a law to make any language official.

In many countries, most of the people have the same native language. This often becomes the official one as well. For example, most people
15   in France speak French as their native language. French is also the official language.

A small country like Zimbabwe can have many official languages. There are four other countries around Zimbabwe, so people speak different
20   languages from those countries. Zimbabwe has the most official languages in the world—sixteen!

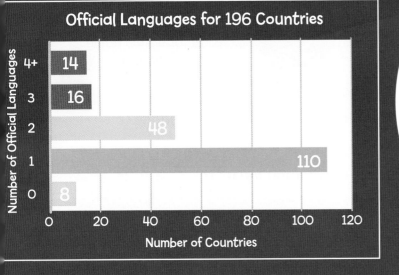

Official Languages for 196 Countries

Number of Official Languages

4+	14
3	16
2	48
1	110
0	8

Number of Countries: 0 20 40 60 80 100 120

English

French

A large country like China may have only a few official languages. China is one of the biggest countries in the world. Every day, people in China use over a hundred languages. But most people just use one Chinese language to talk with each other. It's called Mandarin.

25

India is another huge country. Many people in India speak Hindi. It's a native language. But Hindi and English are the two official languages of India. In fact, people in India speak more than a thousand native languages in all!

30

What information is in the **bar graph** that is not in the text? Circle the words.

WHAT CAN YOU DO? Color the stars.

I can read a bar graph. ★ ★ ★

I can understand all the key words. ★ ★ ★

KEY
★ I need help.
★ ★ I can do this a little.
★ ★ ★ I can do this well.

Understand

Remember!
A **bar graph** shows how much or how many. It may give information not in the text.

A Think about the bar graph and text. Answer the questions and discuss with the class.

1. What information does the bar graph show?

2. What does a country need to do if it wants to have an official language?

3. How many countries have no official language?

4. How does the bar graph help you better understand the text?

B Choose the correct answer.

1. Which is an official language of India?

☐ a. Chinese
☐ b. Hindi
☐ c. Spanish
☐ d. none of the above

2. In the bar graph, which color bar would include Zimbabwe?

☐ a. ▨
☐ b. ▨
☐ c. ▨
☐ d. ▨

3. In the bar graph, which country is included in the bar for *1*?

☐ a. China
☐ b. Mexico
☐ c. Zimbabwe
☐ d. France

4. Where might you *not* use an official language?

☐ a. in government
☐ b. while traveling
☐ c. at home
☐ d. at school

C Ask and answer the questions with a partner.

1. What language do you speak at home? Is it the official language of your country?

2. Do you think it's better for a country to have only one official language, or to have many? Why?

3. What are the official languages of the country you live in?

D Complete the sentences.

> Chinese   English   French   Hindi
>
> Mexican   native speakers   official languages   Spanish

A long time ago, people from Spain brought their language to Mexico. Today,
(1) _____ people speak (2) _____. Similarly, language traveled from
England to the United States, so many people in the United States speak (3) _____.

Most people in the United States and Mexico are (4) _____ of either
English or Spanish. People from all over the world have moved to these countries, too.
People from China brought the (5) _____ language with them. Many people
from India brought (6) _____. People from France brought their native language,
(7) _____.

And yet the United States and Mexico are countries with no (8) _____!
Neither country has passed a law to make one.

E Read and complete the sentences with one, two, or three words.

My Languages

My name is Tawanda. I grew up in a small village in Zimbabwe.
The country has sixteen official languages. My native language is
called Shona, and I also learned English in school. I know a few
words in other languages, but don't speak or read them. When
I was nineteen years old, I moved to Tanzania, a country near
Zimbabwe. English and Swahili are the official languages here.
So I'm learning Swahili now, too.

1. Tawanda moved from _____ to _____ when he was nineteen.

2. His family spoke a _____ called Shona at home.

3. Tawanda speaks _____ and is learning _____

4. Tanzania has two _____ languages.

WHAT CAN YOU DO?   Color the stars.

I can read a bar graph to get
information that's not in
the text.

KEY   ⭐ I need help.

⭐⭐ I can do this a little.

⭐⭐⭐ I can do this well.

Read

READING GOAL: Make Predictions

A prediction is what you think will happen. While you read, use clues in the story and your own knowledge to guess what might happen. Make predictions throughout the story and at the end of the story.

Get Ready

A Read the sentences below. Choose the correct answer.

1. Which sentence is a prediction?

   ☐ a. Darla will do well in school.

   ☐ b. Darla fell asleep on the rug.

2. Ron sent a text message. What will happen next?

   ☐ a. He will send the message.

   ☐ b. His friend will read the message.

B Find the key words in the text. Look up words you don't know in your dictionary.

C Read and listen to the story *So Many Questions*. 🔊 12

So Many Questions

"Can you hold the door?" the girl asked Erico in Italian. "No problem," he replied in English, pushing the door open and holding it there.

5 The girl walked through, carrying a big pile of drawing paper and other supplies. "Hi, I'm Rosa," she said as she struggled to hold onto the supplies. "Are you the new student from Italy?"

"No," he replied. "I mean, I only lived there three months, but yes, I'm new here." "You sound like you 10 have a British accent, but you have an Italian name. Did you live in England, too?" asked Rosa. "Sorry, my friends say I ask a lot of questions. I hope you don't mind. But I speak Italian at home, and I thought you might, too." It was the second day of summer school 15 and Erico's second month in the United States. He enjoyed meeting new people, even if they did ask a lot of questions.

"My name is Portuguese, but my family's from Australia. My dad moved there from Brazil, and my 20 mom's from Portugal ..."

"Oh!" Rosa interrupted. "Do they speak Portuguese and English? Are they bilingual? Are you? Do your parents have Australian accents? Does speaking Portuguese help you learn Italian at all? Wait—why do you
25 sound British?"

Rosa asked all of these questions very quickly and dropped her supplies while she was talking. Erico realized that asking so many questions was Rosa's way of being friendly, and he helped her pick up her paper,
30 paint brushes, and colored pencils.

"Yes, Portuguese did help me learn some Italian," he said. "As for my British accent, do you want to hear a long story?"

What do you think Erico's long story is about? Make a **prediction**.

WHAT CAN YOU DO?   Color the stars.

I can find clues and make predictions about a story. ⭐⭐⭐

I can understand all the key words. ⭐⭐⭐

KEY
⭐ I need help.
⭐⭐ I can do this a little.
⭐⭐⭐ I can do this well.

Understand

A Think about making predictions. Answer the questions and discuss with the class.

1. Read the paragraph starting at line 4. What class do you think Rosa is going to?

2. How did you think Erico would answer Rosa's questions? Did he answer the way you thought he would?

3. Do you think Rosa always talks to new people the way she does to Erico? Why or why not?

4. What do you predict will happen after the story ends?

B Read. Choose **T** for **True** and **F** for **False**.

1. Rosa first speaks to Erico in Portuguese.   T   F
2. Rosa and Erico are studying art.   T   F
3. Erico was born in Australia.   T   F
4. Erico's parents were born in different countries.   T   F
5. Erico decides Rosa is unfriendly.   T   F
6. Knowing Portuguese helped Erico learn Italian.   T   F
7. Erico speaks with an Australian accent.   T   F
8. Erico has a long story to tell Rosa.   T   F

C Ask and answer the questions with a partner.

1. How many languages do you think Erico speaks? Why?

2. What countries do you think Erico has lived in? Why?

3. How do you become friends with a new classmate?

4. Is it friendly to ask a new classmate a lot of questions? Why or why not?

5. Do you think Rosa and Erico will become friends? Why or why not?

D Choose the correct answer.

1. In line 2, *Italian* means a language from
   - ☐ a. Australia.
   - ☐ b. Brazil.
   - ☐ c. Italy.
   - ☐ d. Portugal.

2. In line 10, *accent* means a way to
   - ☐ a. draw or paint.
   - ☐ b. pronounce words.
   - ☐ c. make new friends.
   - ☐ d. ask many questions.

3. In line 18, *Portuguese* means from
   - ☐ a. England.
   - ☐ b. Portugal.
   - ☐ c. Italy.
   - ☐ d. Brazil.

4. In line 22 , *bilingual* means
   - ☐ a. moving a lot.
   - ☐ b. being friendly.
   - ☐ c. pushing a door open.
   - ☐ d. speaking two languages.

E Read the text. Then read the questions and choose the correct answer.

Hey, Friends!

Jane and Tomi, I really miss you, my friends! We'll have to do a video call soon. I miss Mexico, but we're having fun in California. Also, it's nice to speak English again every day. Although some days it's hard to remember which conversations I've had in which language! My sister has already made some new friends—oops, I just sat down to write this, but I hear my dad calling, saying dinner's ready. I'll be back later!

Hello!
Ciao!
Olá!

1. What does the writer want to do soon?
   - ☐ a. write a letter to her family
   - ☐ b. have a video call with friends
   - ☐ c. make dinner for her brother
   - ☐ d. speak with someone in English

2. What will the writer do after sending this message?
   - ☐ a. make new friends
   - ☐ b. call her father
   - ☐ c. have a conversation
   - ☐ d. go eat dinner

WHAT CAN YOU DO? Color the stars.

I can use clues and my own knowledge to make predictions in a story. ★★★

KEY
★ I need help.
★★ I can do this a little.
★★★ I can do this well.

Reading Check

Remember!
Use a **bar graph** to learn more about a text. Find clues that help you make a **prediction**.

A Read and listen.  13

The Life of a Language

A language is *living* as long as people use it every day. Some languages are used a lot, but some are disappearing. Languages that are no longer used are called *dead* languages.

Mandarin, for example, is a living language. It is one of the official languages of China. More people speak Mandarin than any other language in the world. (See the bar graph.)

Latin is an example of a dead language. Some people still speak it, but it is used less and less. It's not an official language in any country.

New languages are always being born, too. For instance, people have created many kinds of sign languages. Australian sign language is different from Portuguese sign language. People make up the languages used to run computers. And sometimes people make up a language just to use it in a book or movie.

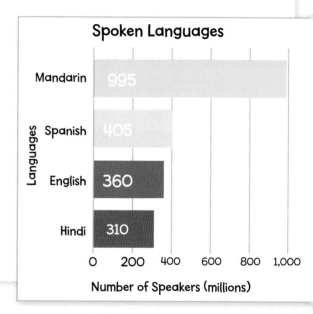

Spoken Languages

Languages	Number of Speakers (millions)
Mandarin	995
Spanish	405
English	360
Hindi	310

Number of Speakers (millions): 0 200 400 600 800 1,000

B Read the text again. Then choose the correct answer.

1. If you can say which language is spoken by about 360 million people, then you can
   - [ ] a. make predictions.
   - [ ] b. understand a bar graph.

2. If you say Mandarin will live a long time, you are
   - [ ] a. making a prediction.
   - [ ] b. understanding a bar graph.

C **Answer the questions and discuss your answers with the class.**

1. What language has the smallest number of speakers? How do you know?

2. What will probably happen if only fifty people speak a language?

D **Complete the sentences.**

1. English is a _____ language.
   - ☐ a. made-up
   - ☐ b. new
   - ☐ c. living
   - ☐ d. Chinese

2. Hindi is spoken by about _____ million people.
   - ☐ a. 310
   - ☐ b. 400
   - ☐ c. 950
   - ☐ d. 360

3. Spanish has fewer speakers than _____ does.
   - ☐ a. Australian
   - ☐ b. English
   - ☐ c. Hindi
   - ☐ d. Mandarin

4. Some people still speak _____ but it is not an official language.
   - ☐ a. English
   - ☐ b. Mandarin
   - ☐ c. Latin
   - ☐ d. Spanish

E **Discuss with a partner.**

1. What languages are spoken in your country?

2. How is a language like a living thing?

3. Is a language that is made up for a movie a living language? Why or why not?

F **Choose the best word.**

Marcel speaks several (1. **languages / bilingual**) very well. His parents are from France, so the family speaks (2. **Italian / French**) at home. They moved to Italy when he was six, where Italian is the (3. **new / official**) language. He grew up there, so he speaks Italian without a French (4. **accent / language**). He's interested in studying (5. **Mandarin / Portuguese**), too, because he wants to live in China some day.

WHAT CAN YOU DO? Color the stars.

I can read a bar graph. ★ ★ ★

I can make a prediction. ★ ★ ★

KEY
★ I need help.
★ ★ I can do this a little.
★ ★ ★ I can do this well.

Get Ready to Write

WRITING GOAL: Write a Review

A review is an opinion about a text or story. It includes an introduction paragraph with a summary, body paragraphs with likes and dislikes, and a conclusion paragraph with final thoughts.

A Read the review. Underline the phrases used for giving examples.

Writing Tip
Use phrases like *for example*, *for instance*, and *such as* to give examples.

Review of *The Stolen Codes*

Introduction — Some books are difficult to translate. A story might work well in one language, but not always in another. For example, you can now get one of my favorite Italian books in English. The title in English is *The Stolen Codes*. But I don't think I can recommend the English version.

Body paragraphs —

The main story is still interesting. Some parts are written well in English. This includes some of my favorite parts, such as when the main character, Drina, discovers that secret codes were stolen from her computer.

However, the English translation of *The Stolen Codes* is missing some important things. For instance, the English writer did not seem to understand how funny Drina is in Italian. She's a little too serious in English.

Conclusion — *The Stolen Codes* will be made into an Australian movie next year. I recommend not reading the English book. Instead, wait to see if the movie is better.

B Discuss the questions with a partner.

1. What did the reviewer like about the English translation of the book?

2. What did the reviewer not like about it?

3. What might people do or not do after reading this review?

4. Think about a book you've read recently. Would you give it a good review? Why or why not

Write

C Think about a book or story you have read. Complete the chart.

Title: _____

Summary	Liked	Disliked	My Recommendation

D Write about the book or story. Use your words from **C**. Choose new words, too.

1. What is the book or story about?

   _____

2. What did you like about it? Why?

   _____

3. What didn't you like about it? Why?

   _____

4. Would you recommend this book? Why or why not?

   _____

Now write your review.

WHAT CAN YOU DO? Color the stars.

I can write a review. ★ ★ ★
I can use phrases to give examples.
★ ★ ★

KEY
★ I need help.
★ ★ I can do this a little.
★ ★ ★ I can do this well.

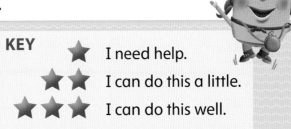

Getting to Know You

MY GOALS

UNIT 9

- Read the story *A Trip to Earth*
- Analyze characters

UNIT 10

- Read the essay *Number 261*
- Understand types of conflict

WRITE

- Write a comparative report

 A Look at the picture.

1. What sports are each of the kids in the picture getting ready to do?

2. Do you play any of these sports? Which ones?

Personalities and Sports

What do the sports you like to play say about you? For instance, if you're more outgoing, you probably like to play team sports like soccer or basketball. If you're quiet, you may prefer an individual sport, like tennis or golf. Do you like to play sports just for fun, or do you always play to win? The games we like to play, and how we play them, can say a lot about our personalities.

B Read the text.

1. What kind of sports do outgoing people probably prefer?

2. What kind of sports do quiet people usually prefer?

3. Are you usually serious or usually laughing? How would you describe yourself?

Think, Pair, Share
Can you describe a good friend? What are they like?

READING GOAL: Analyze Characters

To analyze a character, think about what the character looks like, feels, says, and does. While you read, analyze the characters to help you understand the story.

Get Ready

A Read the sentences below. Choose the correct answer.

1. Which shows surprise?
   - ☐ a. "I can't believe it!"
   - ☐ b. "I can't go today."

2. "Hi. It's nice to see you again," said Alex.
   - ☐ a. Alex is being rude.
   - ☐ b. Alex is being friendly.

3. Which person is happy?
   - ☐ a. Jeff couldn't stop jumping up and down when his team won.
   - ☐ b. Mike stomped his feet and walked away when his team lost.

B Find the key words in the text. Look up words you don't know in your dictionary.

C Read and listen to the story *A Trip to Earth*. 🔊 14

A Trip to Earth

"I don't know how you can be so calm, Nora. After so much time in space, I can't wait to see Earth and smell the air," said Rayyan. He talked almost nonstop all morning to everyone on the shuttle. His twin
5   sister, Nora, knew that Rayyan talked a lot when he was nervous.

Their daring parents left Earth years before with a group of explorers, to live on the planet Regulus. Now Rayyan and Nora were traveling to Earth to visit
10   family that they didn't know very well. The twins were very young the last time they saw their family.

The shuttle landed at last. Nora and Rayyan walked out into a large, open area. Long, colorful pieces of cloth covered the whole space, flapping in the
15   breeze. Hundreds of people walked around or sat at tables, talking.

"Nora and Rayyan! Is that you?" asked a smiling woman walking toward them.

"Hi," said Rayyan. "Yes, I'm Rayyan, and this is Nora.
20   She's the shy one. Sorry, I don't mean to be rude, but I don't remember you."

Nora just smiled and looked thoughtful. "Hi, Irdina," she said.

25 "Shy?" asked Irdina. "I remember Nora being quiet, but confident. And Rayyan, you were always so friendly, I don't think you *can* be rude."

"Oh, our cousin Irdina. I remember you now!" said Rayyan. "I think we were only five when you left for Earth. How are you?"

30 "I'm fine, thanks," she said and hugged them both. "Let's get going. You have a lot of family that can't wait to see you!"

What can you tell about the people in the story? Underline the words that help you **analyze the characters**.

WHAT CAN YOU DO?   Color the stars.

I can analyze characters to help understand the story. ⭐⭐⭐

I can understand all the key words. ⭐⭐⭐

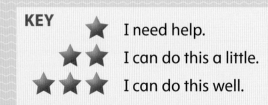

KEY

⭐ I need help.

⭐⭐ I can do this a little.

⭐⭐⭐ I can do this well.

Understand

Remember!
Look for details to help you analyze the characters and **understand the story**.

A Think about analyzing characters. Answer the questions and discuss with the class.

1. How do you know that Rayyan is nervous?

2. What do the other characters say about Nora?

3. Does Irdina already know Nora and Rayyan? How do you know?

4. What else do you know about Rayyan and Nora?

B Choose the correct answer.

1. What did Rayyan do all morning?
   - [ ] a. flew
   - [ ] b. landed
   - [ ] c. smiled
   - [ ] d. talked

2. In the story, how much does Nora talk?
   - [ ] a. once
   - [ ] b. a few times
   - [ ] c. almost nonstop
   - [ ] d. more than Rayyan

3. Why does Rayyan worry that he's being rude?
   - [ ] a. Nora is so quiet.
   - [ ] b. He talks so much.
   - [ ] c. He doesn't remember Irdina.
   - [ ] d. He's never been on Earth before.

4. Why do Rayyan and Nora travel to Earth?
   - [ ] a. for a vacation
   - [ ] b. to visit family
   - [ ] c. for school
   - [ ] d. to smell the air

C Ask and answer the questions with a partner.

1. Are you more like Rayyan or Nora? How?

2. Do you know someone who's quiet, like Nora? Why do you think they're quiet?

3. When could this story take place? How do you know?

4. Have you ever traveled to visit family? How far away did you go?

5. Would you want to travel in space? Where would you go?

D Complete the sentences.

| calm   confident   friendly   daring   nervous   rude   shy   thoughtful |

I get very (1) _____ when I travel by plane. I would like to be more
(2) _____, but I really don't like flying. So when my brother and I went to visit
family last year, we took a train, instead, and I was very (3) _____.

My uncle was so (4) _____. He had a guest room ready for us and made a really
nice dinner. My cousin didn't talk much at first, but I knew he was very (5) _____.

My brother is the (6) _____ one, so when we sat down to dinner, he said to my
cousin, "I don't mean to be (7) _____, but can we switch seats?" My cousin sat
between us and that made it easier for us to talk and get to know each other. After that,
my cousin was much more (8) _____.

E Read and complete the sentences with one, two, or three words.

Family Get-together

The whole Miller family gets together every two years.
Grandparents, parents, and children travel from all over the
country. The grown-ups are friendly, talking a lot the whole
weekend. They plan many activities for the kids so they don't
get bored.

Some kids enjoy quiet activities. The adults make sure they have
crafts to do and games to play. Other kids like to move a lot, so
there are outdoor activities for everyone to do. The older kids
help the younger kids. And everyone has a fun weekend!

1. The Millers get together every _____

2. Some kids like to do _____ activities.

3. The adults make sure these kids have _____ to do and _____ to play.

4. Some kids want to move a lot, so there are _____ _____ for them to do.

WHAT CAN YOU DO? Color the stars.

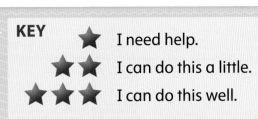

I can analyze characters.

KEY
★ I need help.
★★ I can do this a little.
★★★ I can do this well.

READING GOAL: Understand Types of Conflict

Internal conflicts happen within a character. These conflicts could be about fears or sadness. External conflicts happen outside a character. They could involve other characters or the setting of the story. Identify types of conflict to understand more about the text.

Get Ready

A Read the sentences below. What type of conflict is it? Choose the correct answer.

1. Dan's friend Mark thought it would be funny to hide in the bushes and surprise Dan. But when Mark jumped out and yelled, Dan got very scared.

   ☐ a. external conflict

   ☐ b. internal conflict

2. Dan was afraid to walk past the bushes for a long time after that.

   ☐ a. external conflict

   ☐ b. internal conflict

B Find the **key words in the text.** Look up words you don't know in your dictionary.

C Read and listen to the essay *Number 261.* 🔊 15

Number 261

Kathrine Switzer began running when she was twelve years old. Her father suggested she run one mile (1.2 kilometers) each day, to get fit enough to play for a school team. She 5 discovered that running made her feel strong and fearless.

Switzer was studious. She got good grades in high school and college. She also kept running and found a coach. He ran many times in a race 10 called the Boston Marathon.

Switzer wanted to run a marathon (a 42-kilometer race) but her coach didn't think women could run that far. Switzer was sure he was wrong. She trained until she could run *more* 15 *than* 42 kilometers. Her coach was proud of her and helped her enter the next Boston Marathon.

The night before the race, Switzer rode in a car to see the race route. It seemed like such a long course, and it made her very nervous. She 20 wondered if she would be able to complete the race. But a phone call from her father made her feel brave. He told her that she was strong and that she knew she would run well.

In a marathon, each runner wears a number. Switzer's
25 number in the 1967 Boston Marathon was 261. The people
who organized the race didn't know that a woman was going
to be running. When they saw Switzer wearing the number
261, one of the organizers ran after her and tried to pull her
number off! But he failed and Switzer finished the race.

30 This experience gave Switzer new ideas. She was patient and
worked with other women runners to change the rules. It
took them five years, but now women can run in the Boston
Marathon.

Today Switzer stays busy helping women racers all over the
35 world. She is a generous person, taking time to encourage
other women runners.

What are the
conflicts in the
text? Are they
external or
internal?

WHAT CAN YOU DO? Color the stars.

I can identify conflicts in a story. ★ ★ ★

I can understand all the key words. ★ ★ ★

KEY ★ I need help.

★ ★ I can do this a little.

★ ★ ★ I can do this well.

Understand

A Think about internal and external conflicts. Answer the questions and discuss with the class.

1. What is the first external conflict in the text?

2. What is the internal conflict?

3. How did these conflicts affect Switzer?

4. Have you ever been told you couldn't do something you knew you could do? What did you do?

B Read. Choose **T** for **True** and **F** for **False**.

1. Women have always run the Boston Marathon.   T   F

2. Running made Switzer feel strong.   T   F

3. A marathon is 50 kilometers.   T   F

4. Switzer's coach did not think she could run a marathon.   T   F

5. Switzer started the Boston Marathon without a number.   T   F

6. Switzer helped change the Boston Marathon rules.   T   F

7. Running the marathon gave Switzer new ideas.   T   F

8. After the marathon, Kathrine Switzer never ran again.   T   F

C Ask and answer the questions with a partner.

1. Why do you think the title of the essay is *Number 261*?

2. What made Switzer want to help women runners?

3. Have you ever had to work hard just to take part in something? What was it?

4. Have you felt nervous before a big event? What did you do to stay calm?

5. How would you feel if someone tried to take your number away in a race? Why?

D Choose the correct answer.

1. In line 4, *fit* means
   - ☐ a. sure but scared.
   - ☐ b. good at school.
   - ☐ c. strong and healthy.
   - ☐ d. can wait a long time.

2. In line 7, *studious* means
   - ☐ a. thinks a lot.
   - ☐ b. runs very far.
   - ☐ c. picks a number.
   - ☐ d. works hard in school.

3. In line 22, *brave* means
   - ☐ a. fearless.
   - ☐ b. young.
   - ☐ c. working.
   - ☐ d. new.

4. In line 30, *patient* means
   - ☐ a. learning.
   - ☐ b. asking.
   - ☐ c. calm.
   - ☐ d. running.

E Read the text. Then read the questions and choose the correct answer.

A Helping Hand

One bright spring day, Mario left his house with lots of time to get to his bus for school. Near the bus stop, his backpack fell open and his school supplies spilled everywhere. He was worried he would miss the bus. Mario told himself to stay calm as he started picking things up. Many people hurried past without stopping, but finally, help arrived! One of his classmates, Julian, stopped to help. Mario felt calmer and said "Thanks!" as they ran for the bus.

1. How did Mario feel when his backpack fell open?
   - ☐ a. worried
   - ☐ b. helpful
   - ☐ c. organized
   - ☐ d. calm

2. Which is the best word to describe Julian's actions?
   - ☐ a. spilled
   - ☐ b. calm
   - ☐ c. tall
   - ☐ d. helpful

WHAT CAN YOU DO? Color the stars.

I can identify how a writer uses words to show how characters feel. ★★★

KEY
★ I need help.
★★ I can do this a little.
★★★ I can do this well.

Reading Check

A Read and listen. 🔊 16

The Exercise Question

Yuki liked to play tennis, but he was becoming a little bored with it. He played for several years and even competed in some tournaments. He wanted to stay fit, but he also wanted to try a new sport.

Yuki sometimes went running, but he thought it was a little boring. He thought about trying soccer, but it always took him a while to feel confident in large groups, so he decided not to do a team sport. Then, his thoughtful friend Maya suggested he try swimming. He had a swimsuit and knew how to swim a little.

Yuki asked his mom if he could take swimming lessons. He was nervous, thinking about taking a class with lots of new people. They found lessons for him, and it turned out to be a small group. Yuki had a great time.

B Read the text again. Then choose the correct answer.

1. If you want to learn about Yuki, what should you do?

☐ a. analyze character

☐ b. understand types of conflict

2. What are you doing when you think about problems that characters have in a text?

☐ a. analyzing characters

☐ b. understanding types of conflict

C   **Answer the questions and discuss your answers with the class.**

1. What kind of conflict does Yuki have in choosing a new sport?

2. Why do you think Yuki might be nervous in large groups?

D   **Complete the sentences.**

1. Yuki is _____ on a tennis court.

   ☐ a. confident   ☐ b. friendly

   ☐ c. nervous   ☐ d. young

2. Yuki is most likely _____ when meeting new people.

   ☐ a. busy   ☐ b. cheerful

   ☐ c. shy   ☐ d. unpopular

3. Taking the class even though he's nervous shows Yuki is _____

   ☐ a. unpopular.   ☐ b. studious.

   ☐ c. cheerful.   ☐ d. brave.

4. Yuki wants to try something new and still stay _____

   ☐ a. brave.   ☐ b. studious.

   ☐ c. fit.   ☐ d. busy.

E   **Discuss with a partner.**

1. How well do you think Yuki's friend Maya knows him?

2. How might playing sports help people become confident?

3. Are you more comfortable in small or large groups? Why?

F   **Choose the best word.**

Dear Maya,

Thank you for recommending swimming. It was a very (1. **calm / thoughtful**) suggestion.

As you know, I can be (2. **nervous / studious**) in big groups, but it turned out there were only ten kids in the class! The teacher told us to be (3. **calm / young**) and to keep trying when we're trying to learn new skills. This helped me feel (4. **friendly / brave**).

I'm still (5. **busy / gentle**) with my school schedule, but I always have time for swimming lessons!

Thanks again,

Yuki

WHAT CAN YOU DO?   **Color the stars.**

I can analyze characters in a story. ★ ★ ★

I can understand different kinds of conflict in a text. ★ ★ ★

KEY

★   I need help.

★ ★   I can do this a little.

★ ★ ★   I can do this well.

Get Ready to Write

WRITING GOAL: Write a Comparative Report

A comparative report compares two things. It includes an introduction paragraph, body paragraphs to show how two things are similar and different, and a conclusion paragraph with a strong final thought.

A Read the comparative report. Underline a phrase that shows differences.

Writing Tip
Use phrases like *in contrast* and *on the other hand* to show differences.

Exercise and You

by Darren Brown

Introduction — Many studies show that staying fit is important. Exercise helps your body stay healthy. It helps you sleep well, avoid stress, and be in a good mood, too! But everyone is different. Not everyone enjoys doing the same activities.

How things are similar — Some people feel confident in any situation, and they may enjoy group activities like soccer and baseball. In these activities, they can meet new people, work as a team, and exercise, too!

How things are different — In contrast, some people can be shy. Big groups may make them nervous and they may not enjoy team sports. Running and bicycling are exercise activities you can easily do on your own.

Conclusion — Think about your abilities. How comfortable are you in groups? Then choose the best activity for *you*!

B Discuss the questions with a partner.

1. Which paragraph tells you why exercise is important?

2. How is exercise good for you?

3. What two things are being compared in this report?

4. What does the conclusion recommend people do?

Write

C Think about the personalities of two people you know. What do they like to do? Complete the chart.

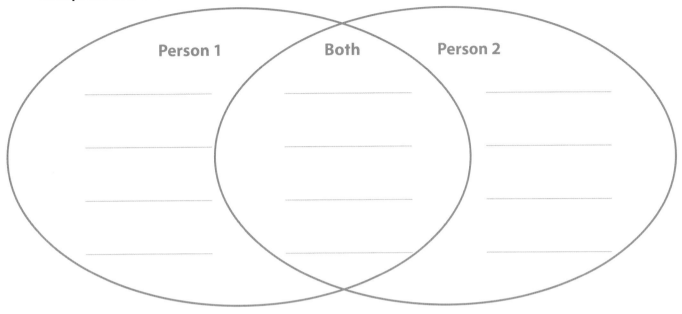

Person 1   Both   Person 2

D Write about your two friends. Use your words from **C**. Choose new words, too.

1. What will you write in your introduction?

2. How are these two people alike?

3. How are these two people different?

4. What will you write for your conclusion?

Now write your comparative report.

WHAT CAN YOU DO? Color the stars.

I can write a comparative report. ⭐⭐⭐

I can write an introduction, body paragraphs, and a conclusion. ⭐⭐⭐

KEY
⭐ I need help.
⭐⭐ I can do this a little.
⭐⭐⭐ I can do this well.

Finding Adventure

MY GOALS

UNIT 11

- Read the story *My Mexican Adventure*
- Make a value judgment

UNIT 12

- Read the article *Adventures in Science*
- Understand a pie chart

WRITE

- Write a research report

A Look at the picture.

1. Where do you think the people in the picture are?

2. What do you think they're doing? Why?

Wanted: Scientists

Do you want to find adventure and see the world? Can you imagine exploring the oceans? Then you should consider a job as an ocean scientist! Take a small boat out to study large sea animals. Or study volcanoes deep underwater and the small animals that live around them. You'll need a love of adventure, and you might get to see places almost no one else has seen. Jump on in. The water is … extremely cold!

B **Read the text.**

1. What is something ocean scientists study?

2. Why is a job as an ocean scientist an adventure?

3. Would you like to study animals deep underwater? Why or why not?

Think, Pair, Share
Have you ever been to the ocean? What things did you see there?

Read

READING GOAL: Make a Value Judgment

Value judgments are opinions about what is right or wrong. While you read, think about a character's words and actions. Ask yourself, *Did the character do the right thing? What kind of person is the character?*

Get Ready

A Read the sentence below. Choose the best answer.

In old English stories, Robin Hood stole from rich people and gave what he stole to poor people.

1. Which could be called *wrong*?

   a. He stole from some people.

   b. He helped some people.

2. Which could be called *right*?

   a. He stole from some people.

   b. He helped some people.

B Find the key words in the text. Look up words you don't know in your dictionary.

C Read and listen to the story *My Mexican Adventure*. 🔊 17

My Mexican Adventure

by Camilla Jensen

I have an adventure list! It's a list of places I want to see and explore. First on my list is the Amazon jungle. Second is Mt. Everest, which is the highest mountain in the world! Third on the list is seeing pyramids.

5　Last summer, my family took a trip to Teotihuacán in Mexico! There's a famous pyramid there called The Pyramid of the Sun. It's the biggest building in Teotihuacán—it's 75 meters tall and 225 meters wide. There are 245 steps, so it was a long climb, but the
10　view from the top was amazing! I was excited to learn about Mexican culture. I learned about the country's history, its weather, and its currency, the peso.

On our first day in Mexico we had a delicious lunch. Suddenly, my dad looked at his watch and yelled,
15　"We're late! The bus is about to leave!" We started running, but then I noticed a man behind us. He was struggling to pull a suitcase, and in his hand was a bus ticket. He looked worried. "Can we help him?" I asked. "I know we might miss the bus." My parents looked
20　at the man. "Yes, Camilla, we can help him," they said. I asked him if we could help with his suitcase. He said thank you over and over again. We were disappointed that we missed the bus but happy that we made a new friend.

Make a value judgment. Why do you think Camilla went kayaking even though she was afraid?

25 On our final day in Mexico, my parents wanted to go kayaking. I was afraid to paddle a boat in the ocean. But kayaking was on my dad's adventure list, so I decided to try. It was scary but fun.

I had a great adventure in Mexico. Maybe next year, we can
30 go rock climbing in one of our country's national parks!

WHAT CAN YOU DO? Color the stars.

I can make value judgments about a character. ⭐⭐⭐

I can understand all the key words. ⭐⭐⭐

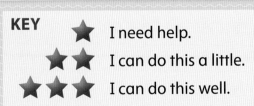

KEY

⭐ I need help.

⭐⭐ I can do this a little.

⭐⭐⭐ I can do this well.

Understand

Remember!
Ask yourself what a character's actions and words show. Do they do the right thing? Why or why not?

A Think about making value judgments. Answer the questions and discuss with the class.

1. Did Camilla do the right thing helping the man with his bags? Why or why not?

2. What can you learn about Camilla in this story?

3. How did the family feel about missing the bus? Why?

B Choose the correct answer.

1. How tall is The Pyramid of the Sun?
   - ☐ a. 225 meters
   - ☐ b. 245 meters
   - ☐ c. 75 meters
   - ☐ d. 150 meters

2. What is Camilla excited to learn about in Mexico?
   - ☐ a. the culture
   - ☐ b. the money
   - ☐ c. the parks
   - ☐ d. kayaking

3. Why does the man look worried?
   - ☐ a. He doesn't have any pesos.
   - ☐ b. He didn't have a bus ticket.
   - ☐ c. He didn't have lunch.
   - ☐ d. His suitcase is very heavy.

4. What did the family do at the ocean?
   - ☐ a. go rock climbing
   - ☐ b. go kayaking
   - ☐ c. go to Teotihuacán
   - ☐ d. go home

C Ask and answer the questions with a partner.

1. Would you like to visit pyramids in Mexico? Why?

2. What country would you like to learn more about? Why?

3. Would you like to go kayaking? Why?

4. Would you like to go rock climbing? Why?

5. Do you have an adventure list? What places do you most want to visit?

D Complete the sentences.

> Amazon   culture   currency   kayaking
>
> Mt. Everest   national park   rock climbing   pyramids

Do you want to climb (1) _____, the world's tallest mountain? Maybe you want to see the (2) _____ in Egypt, or the (3) _____ jungle. Or you could visit a (4) _____ and see nature.

You'll have to learn about the local (5) _____, like what (6) _____ the people use to pay for things. You may want to do some activities, like going (7) _____ in the hills or going (8) _____ on the ocean.

E Read and complete the sentences with one, two, or three words.

Truth and Bicycles

One day Jarred crashed when he was riding his mountain bike. The bike fell one way, and he fell the other. Tim almost laughed, but he didn't want to embarrass Jarred.

"Are you okay?" Tim asked his friend.

"Yes, but I have some big scratches," said Jarred. As Tim got out a first aid kit, Jarred said, "I guess that looked pretty funny, didn't it?"

Tim saw that Jarred was smiling and decided he could tell the truth.

"I'm glad you're okay, but that *was* really funny." They both laughed as Tim handed some bandages to Jarred.

1. Tim thought it looked funny when Jarred _____
2. Tim didn't want to laugh in case it would _____ his friend.
3. Tim got out a _____ to help Jarred with his injuries.
4. In the end, both friends _____ about the event.

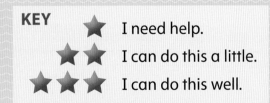

WHAT CAN YOU DO? Color the stars.

I can make value judgments about a character. ★★★

KEY ★ I need help.
★★ I can do this a little.
★★★ I can do this well.

READING GOAL: Understand a Pie Chart

A pie chart is a circle with many pieces. Each piece shows a percentage, and the pieces add up to 100 percent. While you read, look at pie charts to learn more about a topic.

Get Ready

A Read the sentences below. Choose the correct answer.

1. What does each part of a pie chart stand for?
   - ☐ a. less than 100 percent
   - ☐ b. exactly 100 percent

2. What does a whole pie chart stand for?
   - ☐ a. less than 100 percent
   - ☐ b. exactly 100 percent

B Find the key words in the text. Look up words you don't know in your dictionary.

C Read and listen to the essay *Adventures in Science.* 🔊 18

Adventures in Science

When you think of great adventures, you might think of outer space. But you don't have to go to Mars to find adventure. You can visit exciting places right here on Earth! 5 Scientists get to go to amazing places. They can work deep in the ocean or on freezing cold land, like Antarctica.

Antarctica is at the South Pole. It's hard for people to get to, because it's covered in 10 ice all year round. Traveling across the ice is dangerous. So is traveling across the sea around it.

Antarctica is the fifth largest continent in the world. It's bigger than both Europe 15 and Australia. But the human population in Antarctica is tiny. Most of the people who visit are scientists. Some study the mountain ranges under the ice. Others study glaciers, which are like rivers of ice. Very few 20 living things can be found on Antarctica or in the sea around it, but there's enough life for scientists to study.

Size of the Continents

- Australia — 5%
- Europe — 7%
- Antarctica — 9%
- South America — 12%
- North America — 17%
- Asia 30%
- Africa 20%

The deep ocean is another exciting place to study.
25 The bottom of the ocean is a difficult place to get to. It's very dark, and of course you can't breathe underwater. You must also protect yourself from the cold. So it's probably no surprise that we've only seen about
30 five percent of the ocean floor! Scientists find new populations of living things on almost every visit.

Antarctica and the deep ocean are very interesting places. They are also dangerous and difficult places to go. You have to be a very determined person to
35 study them. But these places are worth the trouble of exploring. Scientists learn new things all the time!

What information do you learn about the topic from the **pie chart**?

WHAT CAN YOU DO?   Color the stars.

I can read a pie chart. ★ ★ ★

I can understand all the key words. ★ ★ ★

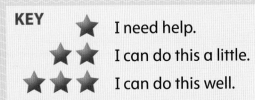

KEY
★ I need help.
★ ★ I can do this a little.
★ ★ ★ I can do this well.

Understand

Remember!
Each piece of a **pie chart** shows a percentage. All the pieces add up to 100 percent.

A Read the pie chart again. Answer the questions and discuss with the class.

1. What percentage of land does Antarctica make up?
2. Which continent is the largest? Which one is the smallest?
3. How many continents are larger than Antarctica? Which ones?
4. What information can you get from the pie chart that isn't in the text?

B Read. Choose **T** for **True** and **F** for **False**.

1. You can find adventure studying science on Earth.   T   F
2. There are few living things in Antarctica.   T   F
3. Antarctica is smaller than Australia.   T   F
4. It is difficult to travel to Antarctica.   T   F
5. A glacier is a thing that lives deep underwater.   T   F
6. Few people who visit Antarctica are scientists.   T   F
7. The ocean floor isn't very cold.   T   F
8. Antarctica is a large percentage of all land on Earth.   T   F

C Ask and answer the questions with a partner.

1. How is traveling to Antarctica like traveling to the deep ocean? How is it different?
2. How would it be difficult to study animals in the deep ocean?
3. Would you want to work in Antarctica? Why or why not?
4. Would you want to be an ocean scientist? Why or why not?

D Choose the correct answer.

1. In line 4, *exciting* means
   - [ ] a. boring.
   - [ ] b. dramatic.
   - [ ] c. cold.
   - [ ] d. hidden.

2. In line 15, *population* means
   - [ ] a. ocean water.
   - [ ] b. dangerous travel.
   - [ ] c. science study.
   - [ ] d. number of people.

3. In line 19, *glaciers* means
   - [ ] a. moving ice.
   - [ ] b. deep water.
   - [ ] c. few people.
   - [ ] d. tall mountain.

4. In line 34, *determined* means a person who will
   - [ ] a. make a choice.
   - [ ] b. study very hard.
   - [ ] c. never give up.
   - [ ] d. be very surprised.

E Read the text. Then read the questions and choose the correct answer.

My Dream Job

My friend, Irma, wants to be an astronaut, but I don't! I think the idea of leaving Earth is too scary. I want to study animals that live near volcanoes in the deep ocean.

Today in class, we learned that astronauts spend time living on the bottom of the ocean! It's part of their training. I guess working on the ocean floor is a little like going to Mars. But I'd rather study amazing ocean animals right here on Earth.

1. What does the writer want to learn about?
   - [ ] a. animals
   - [ ] b. rocks
   - [ ] c. space
   - [ ] d. volcanoes

2. Why doesn't the writer want to be an astronaut?
   - [ ] a. The writer wants to live underwater.
   - [ ] b. The writer thinks Mars is interesting.
   - [ ] c. The writer thinks leaving Earth is scary.
   - [ ] d. The writer thinks space travel is boring.

WHAT CAN YOU DO? Color the stars.

I can understand a pie chart.
⭐⭐⭐

KEY
⭐ I need help.
⭐⭐ I can do this a little.
⭐⭐⭐ I can do this well.

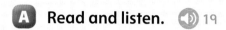

A **Read and listen.** 🔊 19

Math Daydream

Sherman sat in math class. They were learning about pie charts, but he was thinking about the past weekend. On Saturday, he went hiking and fishing with his family. He and his friends planned to go rock climbing on Sunday. They planned to meet in a park near town.

However, on Sunday Sherman woke up late. He was determined to catch up with his friends. He grabbed his climbing equipment and got on his bike. He was in a hurry, but he still took the time to put on his bike helmet.

When Sherman got to the park, no one was there! He thought climbing alone might still be fun. But his parents always warned him never to climb alone, so he decided to go back home. As he was about to leave, his friends arrived. They all slept late, too. Sherman spent the rest of the day rock climbing with his friends.

Back in math class, Sherman imagined a pie chart describing his weekend. His sections included *sleeping*, *hiking,* and *time with friends*.

B **Read the text again. Then choose the correct answer.**

1. When Sherman decided not to climb alone, what was he doing?

   ☐ a. understanding a pie chart

   ☐ b. making a value judgment

2. Sherman imagines "sections" for things he did on the weekend. He can do this because he

   ☐ a. can understand a pie chart.

   ☐ b. can make value judgments.

C Answer the questions and discuss your answers with the class.

1. What kind of person might Sherman be? How can you tell?

2. Based on the text, what activity could Sherman add to his pie chart? Why?

D Complete the sentences.

1. When he imagines his pie chart, Sherman is _____
   - ☐ a. fishing.
   - ☐ b. in math class.
   - ☐ c. biking.
   - ☐ d. hiking.

2. On Sunday, Sherman went _____
   - ☐ a. fishing.
   - ☐ b. hiking.
   - ☐ c. waiting.
   - ☐ d. climbing.

3. Sherman had to find his friends because he _____
   - ☐ a. woke up late.
   - ☐ b. ran outside.
   - ☐ c. was in math class.
   - ☐ d. went hiking.

4. Sherman probably _____ rock climbing with his friends.
   - ☐ a. enjoys
   - ☐ b. forgets
   - ☐ c. describes
   - ☐ d. catches

E Discuss with a partner.

1. How well is Sherman paying attention in math class?

2. What good decisions does Sherman make in the story?

3. Have you ever been late meeting friends? What happened?

F Choose the best word.

Ricky likes to imagine going (1. **rock climbing / kayaking**) on huge rivers. He knows (2. **the Amazon jungle / Antarctica**) has one of the biggest rivers in the world. He hopes to take a boat on it someday.

He also knows some (3. **national parks / glaciers**) in the United States have big rivers. He thinks it would be (4. **exciting / determined**) to ride down them.

Ricky wonders what it would be like to travel across (5. **glaciers / mountain ranges**), which are like frozen rivers. But he knows a boat won't be useful there!

WHAT CAN YOU DO? Color the stars.

I can make a value judgment about a character. ⭐⭐⭐

I can understand a pie chart. ⭐⭐⭐

KEY
⭐ I need help.
⭐⭐ I can do this a little.
⭐⭐⭐ I can do this well.

Get Ready to Write

WRITING GOAL: Write a Research Report

A research report presents information you learn from books, people, or the Internet. It has an introduction with your main idea, body paragraphs with your research, and a conclusion paragraph that summarizes your ideas.

A **Read the report. Underline two synonyms for *brave*.**

Writing Tip

Synonyms are different words with similar meanings. Use synonyms to make your writing more interesting and to avoid repeating the same word.

Nellie Bly

Introduction and main idea

When Nellie Bly was born in 1864, women were almost never allowed to be journalists or travelers. But Bly became both because she was fearless!

Body paragraphs

When she was eighteen years old, Bly read a newspaper article that said women shouldn't have jobs. This made her angry. She wrote a letter to the newspaper explaining why the article was wrong. As a result, they gave her a job!

In 1887, Bly was daring and moved to New York alone. She worked at another newspaper and became famous for her writing.

Bly's next adventure was traveling around the world. She got the idea from a popular book called *Around the World in 80 Days*. Bly's goal was to do the trip in even less time. She was unafraid, and one day in 1899, she left New York by boat. She finished her trip in only 72 days and wrote a book about her adventure!

Conclusion

Nellie Bly was a brave person.

B **Discuss the questions with a partner.**

1. How many body paragraphs does the report have?
2. Why did Bly write a letter to the newspaper?
3. What kinds of work did Bly do?

Write

C Think about something or someone you want to write a research report about. Fill in the chart.

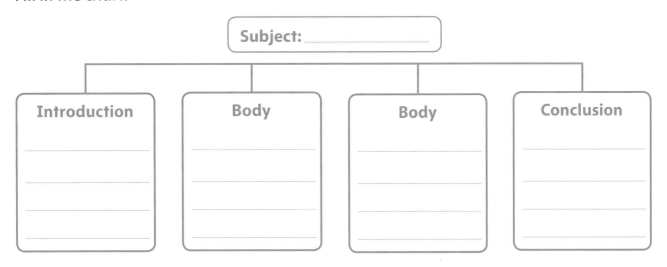

Subject: _____

Introduction	Body	Body	Conclusion

D Write about the thing or person you chose. Use your words from **C**. Choose new words, too.

1. What will your research report be about?

   _____

2. What is the main idea?

   _____

3. What information did you find during your research? How does it support your main idea?

   _____

4. How will you summarize the information for your conclusion?

   _____

Now write your research report.

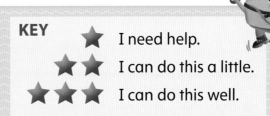

WHAT CAN YOU DO? Color the stars.

I can do research and use it to write a report. ★★★

I can use introduction, body, and conclusion paragraphs to write a research report. ★★★

KEY
★ I need help.
★★ I can do this a little.
★★★ I can do this well.

Reading with Writing 6

Workbook

Renata Brunner-Jass

OXFORD
UNIVERSITY PRESS

Read

READING GOAL:
Identify the Point of View

A Read. Think about who is telling the story while you read.

Review of the City Water Park

My name is Darby and I am ten years old. I visited the City Water Park in August with my family. We had a great time, and I thought all of the play areas were amazing. I really liked the fountains and spent a lot of time running through them. My sister and I had fun spraying water at everyone, especially our parents.

I also liked the huge play pool, but my younger sister, Dina, said it was boring. I thought the big water slides were great! However, Dina was afraid to go on some of them. Sometimes the lines were really long, too.

We all had a great time on the little boats. Overall, I think our favorite activities were the fountains and the boats. We definitely enjoyed our visit to the water park and want to go back again soon!

B Choose the correct answer.

1. The two girls tell the story.
   - [ ] a. true
   - [✔] b. false
   - [ ] c. doesn't say

2. Their mother liked the slides best.
   - [ ] a. true
   - [ ] b. false
   - [ ] c. doesn't say

3. Darby wrote the review.
   - [ ] a. true
   - [ ] b. false
   - [ ] c. doesn't say

4. The girls enjoyed the boats.
   - [ ] a. true
   - [ ] b. false
   - [ ] c. doesn't say

5. Dina thought the big slides were scary.
   - [ ] a. true
   - [ ] b. false
   - [ ] c. doesn't say

6. The parents liked the boats best.
   - [ ] a. true
   - [ ] b. false
   - [ ] c. doesn't say

C Answer the questions. Use full sentences.

1. Who went to the water park?

   Darby and her family went to the water park.

2. What did Dina say was boring?

   _____

3. What was Dina scared of?

   _____

4. What did the girls enjoy about the fountains?

   _____

D Read the text. Choose the correct word to fill each blank.

This Month at the City Aquarium!

Come see the new exhibits at the City Aquarium this month!

Learn to love sharks! A lot of people think sharks are (1) _____. But there's more to know about sharks than sharp teeth. Come discover these (2) _____ animals.

Babies! What has a shell, four legs, and a tail, and is very cute? A baby (3) _____. The babies are here all month!

Visit often! We create a different special (4) _____ every three months. Come learn about a different sea animal each time!

1. ☐ a. boring   ☐ b. exhibits   ☑ c. scary
2. ☐ a. squid   ☐ b. amazing   ☐ c. bored
3. ☐ a. jellyfish   ☐ b. sea turtle   ☐ c. shark
4. ☐ a. exhibit   ☐ b. shark   ☐ c. interesting

E Unscramble and match.

1. fysiljelh •   • a. an animal that swims faster than an octopus

   _____

2. sopuotc •   • b. an animal that moves by pushing water out of its mouth

   _____

3. diuqs •   • c. an animal that changes colors

   _____

Read

READING GOAL:
Make Inferences

A Read. Make inferences while you read.

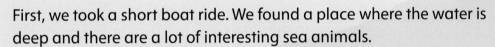

A Snorkling Adventure

by Dan Clark

I went to an amazing water camp last week. We learned a
lot about sea animals. The best part was that we learned
how to swim with a snorkel.

A snorkel is a tube you hold in your mouth and breathe
through when you're underwater. It's fun to swim with your
face underwater!

First, we took a short boat ride. We found a place where the water is
deep and there are a lot of interesting sea animals.

Next, we put on our masks and snorkels, and got in the water! It was
fun, but I swam away when I saw a *garibaldi*. That's a big fish that
looks like giant goldfish. I saw sharks swimming on the bottom, too.

Finally, we were all tired so we went back to camp. The camp leaders
showed us a video they made of us snorkeling. The video was OK, but
I was bored watching it compared to swimming with all the fish!

B Choose the correct answer.

1. What did Dan like best?

☐ a. the boat ride ☐ b. swimming with fish ☐ c. the video

2. What does Dan think is great about using a snorkel?

☐ a. doing a new activity ☐ b. swimming with his face underwater ☐ c. breathing with a tube

3. Why did they need to take a boat ride?

☐ a. get to deeper water ☐ b. see big fish ☐ c. have fun

4. How do you know Dan was scared of the garibaldi?

☐ a. He swam away. ☐ b. He said he was. ☐ c. It was in the video.

C Complete the sentences with one, two, or three words.

1. A snorkel is a tube you put in your mouth and use to _____ breathe.

2. The class took a boat to where _____ was deep.

3. Dan was _____ when he swam near the garibaldi.

4. Dan saw a garibaldi and _____ swimming underwater.

5. Some camp leaders probably didn't go snorkeling since they recorded a _____

6. Dan liked _____ with all the fish the best.

D Choose a word and complete the sentences.

| scared   scary |

1. Dan probably thought the garibaldi were a little _____

2. Dan was not _____ to swim with his face underwater.

| boring   bored |

3. Dan was _____ watching the video.

4. Dan thought the video was more _____ than swimming.

E Read the clues. Write the word.

1. This sea animal has sharp teeth and can be very scary.

_____

2. This is something you make with a camera that you can watch later.

_____

3. This is a person who explores sea life underwater.

_____

Write

Remember!
Use sequencers to show the order of events.

Circle the sequencers. Then look at the sentences below and put them in order.

☐ 1. Next, we took a boat to see the seals.

☐ 2. Then, we got out of the boat and went for a walk on the beach.

☐ 3. First, we had breakfast.

☐ 4. Finally, we went home and took a nap.

Read

READING GOAL:
Identify the Main Idea
and Details

Remember!
A **main idea** is what a
paragraph is about. **Details**
help you understand the
main idea.

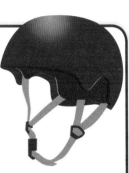

A Read. Look for details that support the main idea.

What Do Helmets Do?

Many people wear a helmet for protection. They can wear them at work or at sports competitions. Firefighters, for example, wear them for work. Baseball players wear them at games. Even kids need to wear helmets when they ride bikes, scooters, or skateboards.

A helmet protects your head. In a fall or a crash, your head may hit the ground. Something could also fall on your head. When accidents like these happen, your helmet will get hit, so your head does not.

Helmets have different shapes and sizes depending on what they're used for. For example, motorcycle helmets are bigger and rounder, covering your whole head. They have see-through covers that protect your eyes from rain and wind. Bicycle helmets are smaller, lighter, and don't cover your face. Most helmets are made of plastic. This lets them be both light and very strong.

B Choose the correct answer.

1. The first paragraph is mainly about why people wear helmets.

   ☐ a. true ☐ b. false ☐ c. doesn't say

2. This is a supporting detail: *Something could also fall on your head.*

   ☐ a. true ☐ b. false ☐ c. doesn't say

3. People sometimes need helmets for medical reasons.

   ☐ a. true ☐ b. false ☐ c. doesn't say

4. Some helmets help protect your eyes.

   ☐ a. true ☐ b. false ☐ c. doesn't say

5. Helmets can be made of leather, metal, or fabric.

   ☐ a. true ☐ b. false ☐ c. doesn't say

6. Bicycle helmets need to be heavier than motorcycle helmets.

   ☐ a. true ☐ b. false ☐ c. doesn't say

C **Answer the questions. Use full sentences.**

1. Why do people wear helmets?

_____

2. How does a helmet protect your head?

_____

3. How does a motorcycle helmet protect your eyes?

_____

4. Why are many helmets made of plastic?

_____

D **Read the text. Choose the correct word to fill each blank.**

Safe Sports

I like to run, so I joined the track team at school. Last week I ran in my first
(1) _____ and finished second! Bicycle racing is a lot of fun, but it can be
dangerous, so you have to wear a (2) _____. I like to go canoeing, too, but
I always wear a (3) _____ in case I fall out of the canoe. You also have to
remember to put on (4) _____, especially on really sunny days. My brother
doesn't like sports very much. His favorite thing to do is to get up really
early and watch (5) _____.

1. ☐ a. competition ☐ b. weather ☐ c. safety
2. ☐ a. helmet ☐ b. sunscreen ☐ c. head
3. ☐ a. sunscreen ☐ b. helmet ☐ c. life jacket
4. ☐ a. gloves ☐ b. sunscreen ☐ c. competition
5. ☐ a. sunscreen ☐ b. a helmet ☐ c. birds

E **Unscramble and match.**

1. rafcs •   • a. protects your head

_____

2. melhte •   • b. protects you from the sun

_____

3. nescnures •   • c. something you wear when you are in a boat

_____

4. feil kacjte •   • d. something you wear around your neck

_____

Read

READING GOAL:
Identify the Main Idea
and Theme

A Read. Look for words that tell you the theme and main idea.

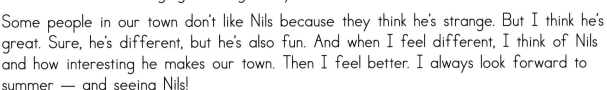

Signs of Summer

When you think of summer starting, you probably think about putting away the scarves and mittens, grass turning green, and trees growing new leaves. In our town, we know it's summer when a certain person appears. His name is Nils.

My friend Tyra says she always sees Nils wearing sunglasses, even when it's cloudy. My friend Kai says Nils wears a new helmet every year. He always wears different clothes that have bright colors. Sometimes he wears a life jacket, even though he's not in a boat! But one thing is always the same. Everywhere he goes, Nils plays a guitar as he skates, and sometimes he's singing as he goes by!

Some people in our town don't like Nils because they think he's strange. But I think he's great. Sure, he's different, but he's also fun. And when I feel different, I think of Nils and how interesting he makes our town. Then I feel better. I always look forward to summer — and seeing Nils!

B Choose the correct answer.

1. **What is the main idea of the story?**
   - ☐ a. Seeing Nils means summer is starting.
   - ☐ b. Playing guitar is fun.
   - ☐ c. Leaves turn green in summer.

3. **What does Nils *always* wear?**
   - ☐ a. scarves and mittens
   - ☐ b. clothes with bright colors
   - ☐ c. a life jacket

2. **What is a sign of summer in this town?**
   - ☐ a. someone shoveling snow
   - ☐ b. someone putting away winter clothes
   - ☐ c. someone playing guitar while skating

4. **What do you learn about the writer by the end of the story?**
   - ☐ a. The writer thinks it's wrong to judge people who are different.
   - ☐ b. The writer doesn't like Nils.
   - ☐ c. The writer wants to learn to play guitar like Nils.

C Complete the sentences with one, two, or three words.

1. When summer weather arrives, trees _____

2. When the weather turns warm, you can put away
   your _____ and _____

3. When you're skating, you should always wear a _____

4. Most people can't _____ while they skate.

5. Nils likes to wear clothes that have _____

6. Nils makes the town _____

D Choose a word and complete the sentences.

| belt | life jacket |

1. You should always wear a _____ when you're in a boat.

2. My father wears a _____ to help carry his tools.

| mittens | a helmet |

3. You wear _____ to help keep you warm.

4. You wear _____ to protect your head.

E Read the clues. Write the word or phrase.

1. This is what you turn in to your teacher at school.

   _____

2. You turn this up when it gets too cold.

   _____

3. If you like to read, you probably have a lot of these.

   _____

4. If the music is too loud, you can do this.

   _____

Write

Remember!
Capitalize the important words in a headline. Always capitalize the first and last word.

Capitalize the first, last, and important words in the headline.

a new adventure park with three ropes courses opens this weekend

Read

READING GOAL:
Identify and Analyze
the Setting

Remember!
The **setting** is when and where a story happens.

A Read. Look for words that tell you about the setting.

Finding the Market

Ana and Perla visit their grandparents every June. They were allowed to walk to the town center by themselves after they turned fifteen. One morning, as they were heading for the farmers' market, they paused at an unfamiliar street corner.

Ana said, "I think we're lost. Maybe we should go back."

Just then, a small woman walked by with an unusual–looking dog. Ana and Perla had never seen a dog like that before.

"Excuse me. How do we get to the town center?" Ana asked the woman. She answered, "Turn right here. It's two blocks west."

They thanked her and turned the corner. Then Ana suddenly stopped.

"Hey, the market's there, across the street! Is something wrong?" asked Perla.

Ana said, "I think that woman was walking with a fox!"

B Choose the correct answer.

1. The story takes place in a big city.
   ☐ a. true   ☐ b. false   ☐ c. doesn't say

2. Ana and Perla are sisters.
   ☐ a. true   ☐ b. false   ☐ c. doesn't say

3. Ana and Perla don't know the town very well.
   ☐ a. true   ☐ b. false   ☐ c. doesn't say

4. Perla calls her grandparents to get directions.
   ☐ a. true   ☐ b. false   ☐ c. doesn't say

5. Ana and Perla find the market.
   ☐ a. true   ☐ b. false   ☐ c. doesn't say

6. The woman who gives them directions is walking a dog.
   ☐ a. true   ☐ b. false   ☐ c. doesn't say

C Answer the questions. Use full sentences.

1. How do Ana and Perla get to the market?

_____

2. Where is the farmers' market?

_____

3. What do the girls see after they turn the corner?

_____

4. What did Ana see walking with the woman?

_____

D Read the text. Choose the correct words to fill each blank.

The Directions

Welcome to our Treasure Hunt! Start by standing (1) _____ the swings.
Go (2) _____ for fifty steps. Now (3) _____ and look for three trees standing
together. Walk until you're standing (4) _____ them. Finally, read your
(5) _____ to find the treasure! After you find it, please (6) _____ to the
picnic tables.

1. ☐ a. run fast   ☐ b. read a map   ☐ c. next to
2. ☐ a. up   ☐ b. straight   ☐ c. between
3. ☐ a. turn right   ☐ b. go back   ☐ c. play
4. ☐ a. between   ☐ b. around   ☐ c. on the left
5. ☐ a. hill   ☐ b. map   ☐ c. tree
6. ☐ a. straight   ☐ b. next to   ☐ c. go back

E Unscramble and match.

1. og ckab •

_____

2. og tshigtar •

_____

3. wentbwe •

_____

• a. in the middle of

• b. return

• c. continue in the same direction

Read

READING GOAL:
Use Visuals

> **Remember!**
> **Visuals** like pictures, diagrams, and maps give you information to help you understand the ideas in a text.

A Read. Use the visual and the text to answer the questions.

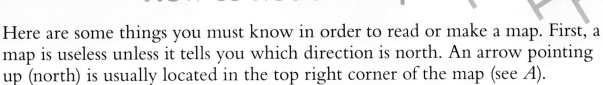

How to Read a Map

Here are some things you must know in order to read or make a map. First, a map is useless unless it tells you which direction is north. An arrow pointing up (north) is usually located in the top right corner of the map (see *A*).

Every map should also have a scale. A scale tells you what a distance on the map stands for in the real world. For example, this scale (see *B*) shows that 1 centimeter on the map stands for 1,000 centimeters, or 10 meters, in the real world.

A map should also have a key that explains signs used on the map (see *C*). For example, a school is often shown by a square with a flag on top. The sign for a hospital is usually a capital H in a blue square. Green trees are used to show a park.

Now try making a map of your own! What else will you include on it?

N ▲ (A)
(C)
Hospital   H
Post office   ✉
School   🏫
Libary   📖

(B) SCALE 1:1000

B Choose the correct answer.

1. Where is the north arrow on the map?
   - ☐ a. the center
   - ☐ b. the top right corner
   - ☐ c. next to the legend

2. What is one thing a map must show you?
   - ☐ a. centimeters
   - ☐ b. a flag
   - ☐ c. north

3. What does a map scale tell you about?
   - ☐ a. arrows
   - ☐ b. distances
   - ☐ c. places

4. What's the sign for *library*?
   - ☐ a. a square with flag
   - ☐ b. an open book
   - ☐ c. a square with a capital H

C Complete the sentences with one, two, or three words.

1. Three things that help you _____ are the north arrow, the scale, and the key.

2. The house with a flag on top shows a _____ and it's across the street from the _____

3. The blue square with the capital H shows a _____

4. The map shows that the post office is _____ the street from the library.

5. _____ are used to show a park.

6. There's a _____ next to the school.

D Choose a word and complete the sentences.

next to	in front

1. You would probably see a mailbox _____ of a post office.

2. The school is _____ a park.

around	cross

3. I run _____ the park for exercise.

4. I look both ways before I _____ the street.

E Read the clues. Write the word or phrase.

1. This word means where two streets meet.

_____

2. This word means at the back of someone or something.

_____

3. This means the same as on the other side of the street.

_____

Write

Remember!
Use phrases like *so that* and *in order to* to show the purpose of an instruction.

Circle the words that show the purpose of an instruction.

Tips for Locking Up Your Bike

In order to keep your bike safe, always take a lock when you travel by bike. Use this so that you can lock the bike to a pole, a bike stand, or anything that cannot be moved.

Read

**READING GOAL:
Understand a Bar
Graph**

Remember!
A **bar graph** compares two
things and shows how many
or how much. It can give
information not in the text.

A Read. Look at the bar graph and read the text.

The Beautiful Game

Do you know what the most popular sport in the world is?
Here's a hint — it's played with a black-and-white ball. Players
kick it around a big grass field. You probably know what sport
this is, but do you know what we call it in English? It depends
on where you live.

Most native speakers of English call this sport *football*. Most
languages around the world also call it that, but they use their
own words for *foot* and *ball*. For example, in Spanish it's *futbol*
and in Hindi it's *futabol*.

In North America, the sport is called *soccer*. Some African
countries use *soccer* and so does Australia, but it's spelled and
pronounced a little differently. In South Africa, it's spelled *sokker*.
And in New Guinea, it's spelled *soka*.

Football fans have one other term to describe the sport they love:
they call it The Beautiful Game.

**What It's Called in
the 25 Most Common
Languages**

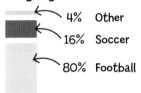

4% Other

16% Soccer

80% Football

B Choose the correct answer.

1. Most English speakers call the sport *soccer*.

　☐ a. true 　　☐ b. false 　　☐ c. doesn't say

2. The word *soccer* is spelled the same everywhere.

　☐ a. true 　　☐ b. false 　　☐ c. doesn't say

3. The game is played with a ball on a grass field.

　☐ a. true 　　☐ b. false 　　☐ c. doesn't say

4. Many Chinese languages have a word that means the same as *football*.

　☐ a. true 　　☐ b. false 　　☐ c. doesn't say

5. The game is called *soccer* in 80 percent of the most common languages.

　☐ a. true 　　☐ b. false 　　☐ c. doesn't say

6. The Beautiful Game is the most popular sport in the world.

　☐ a. true 　　☐ b. false 　　☐ c. doesn't say

C **Answer the questions. Use full sentences.**

1. What are two English words for The Beautiful Game?

    _____

2. What percentage of the most common languages call the sport *football*?

    _____

3. What color in the graph shows the percentage of languages that use the word *soccer*?

    _____

4. What words do the Spanish and Hindi languages use for the sport?

    _____

D **Read the text. Choose the correct word to fill each blank.**

A Simple Game

Native (1) _____ of every language have a name for The Beautiful Game.
In (2) _____, we call it either *football* or *soccer*.

The first football competitions between countries were held in France.
So (3) _____ became an official (4) _____ for these tournaments.

Of course, every country has its own name for the sport. For instance,
if you're in Spain, you would use the (5) _____ word, *futbol*. But it doesn't
matter what you call it or where you live. It's a simple game to play —
you really just need a ball and some friends!

1. ☐ a. people ☐ b. players ☐ c. speakers
2. ☐ a. French ☐ b. English ☐ c. Spanish
3. ☐ a. Spanish ☐ b. French ☐ c. English
4. ☐ a. speaker ☐ b. game ☐ c. language
5. ☐ a. English ☐ b. Spanish ☐ c. French

E **Unscramble and match.**

1. Sipnhas •   • a. the language most people speak in India

    _____

2. Hniid •   • b. the language most people speak in Mexico

    _____

Read

READING GOAL:
Make Predictions

Remember!
Use clues in the story and your own knowledge to make **predictions**.

A Read. Look for words that tell you what will happen next.

Talking in Space

Keenan learned new languages easily. His parents were both bilingual. They spoke New English and Old Portuguese. Keenan could speak more languages, even the main language of Mars! The people there spoke many different languages, but most of them used the official Martian language. It sounded like Hindi to him, another Old Earth language.

One summer, Keenan and his family took a vacation to Mars. On the ship there, they met many different people. He heard accents that he knew but many others that he didn't know. Still, Keenan was the best speaker of the Martian language on the ship.

One day the captain gave Keenan an old book. It had words in two languages. One was English and the other was a language the captain didn't know. The words were in two columns on each page. It also had pictures and diagrams. The captain asked Keenan if he could read the book.

Keenan smiled and turned to the captain. He knew that the book was a Martian dictionary. He also knew just what to do with it!

B Choose the correct answer.

1. What do you think Keenan will do with the book?
   - [ ] a. use it to learn Portuguese
   - [ ] b. show it to his parents
   - [ ] c. teach the captain the Martian language

2. What language do Keenan's parents *not* speak?
   - [ ] a. Portuguese
   - [ ] b. Hindi
   - [ ] c. English

3. What does the Martian language sound like to Keenan?
   - [ ] a. English
   - [ ] b. Portuguese
   - [ ] c. Hindi

4. What language did Keenan speak better than anyone on the ship?
   - [ ] a. English
   - [ ] b. Martian
   - [ ] c. Hindi

C Complete the sentences with one, two, or three words.

1. Keenan can learn new _____ easily.

2. Most people on Mars speak _____ language.

3. Keenan heard many new _____ on the ship.

4. Keenan's parents speak two languages. They are _____

5. Keenan is the _____ of the Martian language on the ship.

6. The captain gives Keenan a _____ that has
   two _____

D Choose a word and complete the sentences.

| native speaker | bilingual |

1. People who speak English and Spanish are _____

2. If you were born in France, you are a _____ of French.

| Portuguese | official language |

3. The language spoken in Brazil and Portugal is _____

4. Mandarin is the _____ of China.

E Read the clues. Write the word.

1. This is the way a person from a place or a country speaks a language.

   _____

2. This word means someone from Great Britain.

   _____

3. This is a large country in South America.

   _____

> **Remember!**
> In a review, use phrases like *for example*, *for instance*, and *such as* to give examples.

Write

Circle the phrases that show examples in the review.

I'm going to tell you about a new book I read, *The Clocks*. It's about a scientist who invents great things, such as a clock that can stop time! There are some good things about it. For instance, it's well written and has great pictures, but I didn't like some of the characters. For example Mr. Maldo, the scientist's friend, seems very rude.

Overall *The Clocks* is easy and fun to read. I highly recommend it!

Read

READING GOAL:
Analyze Characters

A Read. Look for details that help you analyze a character.

A Little Storm

My little sister Alexa may be only six, but she's like a windstorm. I don't think she's ever calm. To her, *everything* is a Big Deal, whether it's good or bad. So when I heard her making noise as she ran around the house this morning, I didn't pay much attention. I thought she was just entertaining herself.

A little while later, I realized the house was very quiet. I became nervous and was about to go find her when she exploded out of the kitchen. I heard her running from one room to another yelling something about glitter. So I asked her what she was doing.

"Jack, I need the glue! It's Mom's birthday tomorrow, and I'm making her a card. Hey, we should make it from both of us!"

Alexa is actually a very fun and thoughtful person. She's also very dramatic!

We found the glue in her room, then went to the kitchen to work on the card.

B Choose the correct answer.

1. Alexa is always quiet.

☐ a. true ☐ b. false ☐ c. doesn't say

2 Jack is a quiet person.

☐ a. true ☐ b. false ☐ c. doesn't say

3. Alexa is frustrated when she can't find the glue.

☐ a. true ☐ b. false ☐ c. doesn't say

4. Alexa is trying to do something nice for her mom.

☐ a. true ☐ b. false ☐ c. doesn't say

5. Jack is happy to help his sister.

☐ a. true ☐ b false ☐ c. doesn't say

6. Jack and Alexa will bake a cake.

☐ a. true ☐ b. false ☐ c. doesn't say

C **Answer the questions. Use full sentences.**

1. What does Jack mean when he compares his sister to a windstorm?

_____

2. Why does Jack begin to wonder about what Alexa is doing?

_____

3. What does Alexa do that is thoughtful?

_____

4. How is Jack helpful to his sister?

_____

D **Read the text. Choose the correct word to fill each blank.**

A Tip

Have you ever worked as a babysitter? Some people are (1) _____ the first time they watch younger children. Don't worry! The parents must be (2) _____ that you can do a good job, or they wouldn't ask you to babysit. Believe in yourself!

Children can get bored easily, so keep them (3) _____. Offer to read to them or to play a game. Both (4) _____ and outgoing kids will talk more if you do activities they like.

1. ☐ a. daring   ☐ b. nervous   ☐ c. thoughtful
2. ☐ a. confident   ☐ b. friendly   ☐ c. busy
3. ☐ a. busy   ☐ b. thoughtful   ☐ c. studious
4. ☐ a. polite   ☐ b. daring   ☐ c. shy

E **Unscramble and match.**

1. rnigda •   • a. not polite or friendly

_____

2. irnldyef •   • b. not easily scared or upset

_____

3. mlac •   • c. brave

_____

4. deur •   • d. kind and helpful

_____

Read

READING GOAL:
Understand Types
of Conflict

> **Remember!**
> **External conflicts** happen outside a character, and **internal conflicts** happen inside a character.

A Read. Look for words that tell you about conflicts the character has.

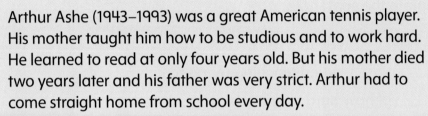

Arthur Ashe

Arthur Ashe (1943–1993) was a great American tennis player. His mother taught him how to be studious and to work hard. He learned to read at only four years old. But his mother died two years later and his father was very strict. Arthur had to come straight home from school every day.

Ashe started playing tennis a year after his mother died and it helped him with his feelings of sadness. His coach, Robert Johnson, taught Ashe how to act on the court. Ashe became famous for being polite and calm. Everyone he played against liked and respected him.

Ashe was the first African-American man to win important tournaments in college and then as a professional. He won tournaments all over the world.

After he retired, Ashe helped young tennis players. Every year, a special event called Arthur Ashe Kids' Day takes place. It's held at an arena named Arthur Ashe Stadium in his honor.

B Choose the correct answer.

1. What is an example of an internal conflict?
   - [ ] a. Arthur's mother died.
   - [ ] b. Arthur felt sadness.
   - [ ] c. Arthur was always calm.

2. When did Ashe start playing tennis?
   - [ ] a. as a teenager
   - [ ] b. in college
   - [ ] c. when he was very young

3. What did Robert Johnson teach Ashe to do?
   - [ ] a. be polite and calm
   - [ ] b. play tennis
   - [ ] c. study and work hard

4. Who did Ashe work with after he finished playing tennis?
   - [ ] a. young tennis players
   - [ ] b. professional tennis players
   - [ ] c. tennis coaches

C Complete the sentences with one, two, or three words.

1. Arthur Ashe's mother taught him to be _____ and to _____

2. Robert Johnson taught Ashe how to be _____ and _____

3. Ashe played tennis in college and then as a _____

4. Ashe won many _____ all over the world.

5. After he retired, Ashe helped _____

6. A special event and a _____ are named after him.

D Choose a word and complete the sentences.

| patient   proud |

1. Alisha is very _____ when teaching tennis to kids.

2. She is _____ of how hard they work.

| brave   busy |

3. People often get tired when they are too _____

4. Being _____ means doing something even if you're afraid.

E Read the clues. Write the word.

1. This word describes someone who works hard and does well in school.

_____

2. This word means being strong and healthy.

_____

Write

Read the text, then choose the correct answer.

Jenna is usually very shy. In contrast, her sister Mindy is comfortable meeting new people. Mindy also likes to read mystery stories. On the other hand, Jenna enjoys adventure stories.

What two things does the text compare?

- [ ] a. what the sisters look like
- [ ] b. how the sisters are different
- [ ] c. what sports the sisters play

Remember!
Use phrases like *in contrast* and *on the other hand* to show differences.

Read

READING GOAL:
Make a Value Judgment

Remember!
Value judgments are opinions about what is right or wrong. As you read the text, ask yourself, *Did the character do the right thing?*

A Read. Look for details that help you make a value judgment.

A Trip to Chichén Itzá

by Sandra Rey

Chichén Itzá is a very old city in Mexico. It was built by people of the Mayan culture. It's famous for its great pyramids.

After the Maya left more than a thousand years ago, grass and other plants grew over a lot of the old city. About a hundred years ago, tourists began to visit the city. Today, more than a million people visit each year. Last year, my parents and I went to see Chichén Itzá!

Before our trip, I learned everything I could about the city. I read that you cannot climb the main pyramid, because it's been damaged from too many tourists climbing it. When we got to the main pyramid, I saw two kids climbing on it! I explained the rules, and they climbed down.

One good thing is that you can climb *some* pyramids. There are also other buildings and nature trails. Chichén Itzá is an amazing place!

B Choose the correct answer.

1. Sandra did the right thing when she explained the rules to the kids.

    ☐ a. true   ☐ b. false   ☐ c. doesn't say

2. People lived in Chichén Itzá about a hundred years ago.

    ☐ a. true   ☐ b. false   ☐ c. doesn't say

3. People from many different countries visit Chichén Itzá.

    ☐ a. true   ☐ b. false   ☐ c. doesn't say

4. Sandra researched the city before seeing it.

    ☐ a. true   ☐ b. false   ☐ c. doesn't say

5. You can't climb any of the pyramids in Chichén Itzá.

    ☐ a. true   ☐ b. false   ☐ c. doesn't say

6. Sandra didn't like Chichén Itzá very much.

    ☐ a. true   ☐ b. false   ☐ c. doesn't say

C Answer the questions. Use full sentences.

1. How many people visit Chichén Itzá every year?

_____

2. Was it a good idea for Sandra to learn about the city? Why?

_____

3. Why can't you climb the main pyramid?

_____

4. Did Sandra do the right thing in telling the kids to climb down?

_____

D Read the text. Choose the correct word to fill each blank.

Adventure Survey!

Describe an adventure you went on. Did your family travel recently? Maybe you got to use a new (1) _____. Perhaps you tried food from a (2) _____ that was new to you.

You can probably imagine even bigger adventures. Many people want to see (3) _____ or other famous buildings. Others want to go (4) _____ or do a different water activity. Maybe camping in a (5) _____ is your favorite thing. Whatever adventures you like, please take a minute to fill out our short survey. Thanks!

1. ☐ a. climb ☐ b. currency ☐ c. jungle
2. ☐ a. pyramid ☐ b. park ☐ c. culture
3. ☐ a. the Amazon ☐ b. pyramids ☐ c. Mt. Everest
4. ☐ a. for a walk ☐ b. kayaking ☐ c. on vacation
5. ☐ a. national park ☐ b. travel ☐ c. pyramid

E Unscramble and match.

1. ruceyncr •   • a. a sport usually done on a river or lake

_____

2. nkgayika •   • b. a large area of land with trees and rivers

_____

3. tanolian kpra •   • c. the kind of money used in a country

_____

Read

READING GOAL:
Understand a Pie Chart

> **Remember!**
> Each part of a **pie chart** shows a percentage, and the parts add up to 100 percent.

A Read. Look for words that tell you how the text and pie chart work together.

Where Do You Want to Go?

Dear Class,

As you know, we sent a survey to all students in our grade. We asked you about the places you want to visit someday. This report and the pie chart show that most of you want to have an adventure!

Some students think hiking on a glacier in Antarctica would be exciting. Others think kayaking in the Grand Canyon would be the most fun. And a lot of students want to become scientists or astronauts and go to Mars! There's been news about plans to visit the planet. But that probably won't happen very soon.

Many students want to explore nature in a place like the Amazon jungle. Others want to go high in the mountains.

We thought that most students want to find adventures close to home. But we were surprised that so many want jobs as scientists in amazing places all over the planet!

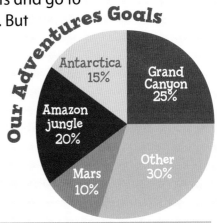

Our Adventures Goals

Antarctica 15%
Grand Canyon 25%
Amazon jungle 20%
Mars 10%
Other 30%

B Choose the correct answer.

1. Which has the greatest value in the pie chart?
   - ☐ a. Mars
   - ☐ b. Grand Canyon
   - ☐ c. Other

2. What does the report tell about the students?
   - ☐ a. They want to have adventures.
   - ☐ b. They don't want to study nature.
   - ☐ c. They like being on Earth.

3. What does the survey ask about?
   - ☐ a. kinds of jobs
   - ☐ b. learning about nature
   - ☐ c. places to visit

4. Which has the least value in the pie chart?
   - ☐ a. Antarctica
   - ☐ b. Mars
   - ☐ c. the Amazon jungle

C Complete the sentences with one, two, or three words.

1. A _____ was given to every student in the grade.

2. The teacher shared the results using a report and a _____

3. Many people want to go kayaking in the _____

4. Fifteen percent of students said they wanted to visit _____

5. Some students want to _____, but that won't happen very soon.

6. The report writers were _____ at some survey results.

D Choose a word and complete the sentences.

glacier	mountain range

1. A _____ is made of ice that moves.

2. A _____ is made of rock and may be covered in ice in winter.

determined	exciting

3. Rock climbing and kayaking are _____ activities.

4. A _____ person can travel to a lot of amazing places.

E Read the clues. Write the word or phrase.

1. This place is very dark, cold, and hard to get to.

_____

2. This word means all the people who live somewhere.

_____

3. This is a country at the South Pole.

_____

4. One day, there might be spaceships so you can do this.

_____

Write

Remember!
Use synonyms to make your writing more interesting and to avoid repeating the same word.

Read the paragraph. Look at the underlined words. Which set of words could you use to make the paragraph more interesting?

I have a new bike! It is <u>big</u> compared to my old bike. The wheels are <u>bigger</u>. I feel like a <u>big</u> kid when I ride it, too!

☐ a. little, smaller, tiny

☐ b. beautiful, fast, great

☐ c. giant, larger, huge

Dictionary

Definitions based on the *Oxford Basic American Dictionary for Learners of English.*

A

above *prep.* in a higher place; higher than someone or something

accent *noun* the way a person from a certain place or country speaks a language

across *prep.* on the other side of something: *across the street from the bookstore*

act *verb* to pretend to be someone else in a play, movie, or television program

along *prep.* from one end of something toward the other end: *along a river*

a lot of *adj.* a large number or amount of things or people

amazing *adj.* very surprising and difficult to believe

Amazon jungle *noun* a large, thick forest in a hot part of South America

Antarctica *noun* the continent around the South Pole

around *adverb* in or to different places or in different directions

Australia *noun* a large island country and continent in the southern Pacific Ocean

Australian *adj.* from or connected with the country Australia

B

behind *prep.* at or to the back of someone or something

belt *noun* a long piece of cloth or leather that you wear around the middle of your body

between *prep.* in the space in the middle of two things or people

bilingual *adj.* able to speak two languages very well

bird *noun* an animal with feathers and wings

block *noun* a group of buildings with streets all around it

bored *adj.* not interested; unhappy because you have nothing interesting to do

boring *adj.* not interesting

bottom *noun* the lowest part of something: *the bottom of the ocean*

brave *adj.* ready to do dangerous or difficult things without fear

Brazil *noun* a country in South America

British *adj.* connected with the United Kingdom of Great Britain and Northern Ireland or the people who live there

busy *adj.* with a lot of things that you must do; working or not free

C

calm *adj.* quiet and not excited or afraid

Chinese *adj.* from or connected with the country China

competition *noun* a game or test that people try to win

confident *adj.* sure that you can do something well, or that something will happen

corner *noun* a place where two lines, walls, or roads meet

cross *verb* to go from one side of something to the other: *cross the street*

culture *noun* the customs, ideas, and way of life of a group of people or a country

D

daring *adj.* not afraid to do dangerous things

determined *adj.* very sure that you want to do something

diver *noun* a person who goes underwater using special equipment

E

English *noun* the language that is spoken in the U.S., Canada, Britain, Australia, etc.

exciting *adj.* making you have strong feelings of happiness and enthusiasm

exhibit *noun* an object or a group of objects that are arranged in a museum, etc. so that people can look at them

F

fearless *adj.* not afraid of anything

fit *adj.* healthy and strong

French *noun* the language of France and some other countries

friendly *adj.* kind and helpful

G

generous *adj.* always ready to give people things or to spend money

glacier *noun* a large area of ice that moves slowly down a mountain: *glaciers*

go back *phrasal verb* to return to a place where you were before

H

hill *noun* a high piece of land that is not as high as a mountain: *up the hill*

Hindi *noun* one of the official languages of India

hurry *verb* to move or do something quickly

I

in front of *prep.* farther forward than another person or thing

interesting *adj.* a person or thing that is interesting and makes you want to know more about them

Italian *noun* the language of the country Italy

J

jellyfish *noun* an animal with a soft, pale body that lives in the ocean. They have long, thin parts that hang down and can hurt (or sting) you.

K

kayak *noun* a light, narrow boat for one person, which you move through the water using a piece of wood with a flat part at each end (called a paddle)

kayak *verb* to travel in a kayak: *go kayaking*

L

left *noun* the left side or direction: *on the left*

M

Mars *noun* the planet that is fourth in order from the sun and second nearest to the earth: *go to Mars*

Mexican *adj.* from or connected with the country Mexico

mitten *noun* a thing that you wear to keep your hand warm. It has one part for your thumb and another part for your other fingers.

mountain range *noun* a line of mountains

Mt. Everest *noun* a mountain in Asia that is the highest mountain in the world

N

national park *noun* a large area of beautiful land that is protected by the government so that people can enjoy it

native speaker *noun* a person who speaks a language as their first language

nervous *adj.* worried or afraid

next to *prep.* at the side of someone or something; beside

O

octopus *noun* an ocean animal with a soft body and eight long arms (called tentacles)

official language *noun* the language used by the government of a country

P

patient *adj.* able to stay calm and not get angry when you are waiting for something, or when you have problems

population *noun* the number of people who live in a place

Portuguese *adj.* from or connected with the country Portugal

proud *adj.* pleased about something that you or others have done or about something that you have

pyramid *noun* a building with a flat bottom and three or four sides that come to a point at the top

R

read *verb* to look at words or symbols and understand them: *read a lot of books/read a map*

rock climb *verb* to climb large rocks or the side of a mountain, usually by using ropes and special equipment: *go rock climbing*

rude *adj.* not polite

S

scared *adj.* afraid

scarf *noun* a piece of material that you wear around your neck to keep warm

scary *adj.* making you feel afraid

seal *noun* an animal with short fur that lives in and near the ocean, and that eats fish

sea turtle *noun* an animal that lives in the sea and has a hard shell on its back

shark *noun* a big fish that lives in the ocean. They have sharp teeth and are often dangerous.

shy *adj.* not able to talk easily to people you do not know

Spanish *noun* the language of Spain, Mexico, and most countries in South America

squid *noun* an animal that lives in the ocean. It has a soft body and ten long parts (called tentacles).

straight *adv.* moving in a way that does not curve: *go straight*

strong *adj.* a strong person has a powerful body and can carry heavy things

studious *adj.* a studious person spends a lot of time studying

sunscreen *noun* a cream that you put on your skin to protect it from the sun

T

take off *phrasal verb* to remove clothes, jewelry, or something else from your body: *take off your watch*

thoughtful *adj.* thinking carefully

turn *verb* to move in a different direction: *turn right/ turned right*

turn down *phrasal verb* to make something produce less sound or heat by moving a switch: *turn down the music*

turn in *phrasal verb* to give your work to a teacher: *turn in your homework*

turn off *phrasal verb* to move the handle or switch that controls something, so that it stops: *turn off the TV/turn off the computer*

turn up *phrasal verb* to make something produce more sound or heat by moving a switch: *turned up the heat*

U

unafraid *adj.* not afraid or nervous

V

video *noun* a short movie or recording of an event that you can watch on a computer, phone, or television

W

watch *verb* to look at someone or something for some time: *watch birds*

wear *verb* to have clothes, jewelry, etc. on your body: *wear a helmet/life jacket*

Syllabus

Topic	Unit	Reading Goal	Key Words	Writing Goal
TOPIC 1 What's in the Water?	Unit 1	Identify the point of view	*octopus, interesting, squid, exhibit, jellyfish, amazing, boring, sea turtle*	Write a detailed description
	Unit 2	Make inferences	*diver, video, bored, seal, shark, scared, scary, tired*	Focus: Sequencers
TOPIC 2 What to Wear	Unit 3	Identify the main idea and details	*turn off the TV, competition, watch birds, wear a helmet, wear a life jacket, take off your watch, scarf, put on sunscreen*	Write a magazine article
	Unit 4	Identify the main idea and theme	*act in a play, read a lot of books, turn in your homework, turn up the heat, belt, mitten, turn down the music, turn off the computer*	Focus: Headline, pictures, and hook
TOPIC 3 From Here to There	Unit 5	Identify and analyze the setting	*on the left, turn right, go straight, next to, go back, up the hill, read a map, between*	Write a process essay
	Unit 6	Use visuals	*corner, go two blocks, across the street from, around, in front of, behind, cross the street, along a river*	Focus: Phrases that show purpose
TOPIC 4 A World of Words	Unit 7	Understand a bar graph	*native speaker, official language, Spanish, Mexican, French, Chinese, Hindi, English*	Write a review
	Unit 8	Make predictions	*Italian, British, accent, Portuguese, Australia, Brazil, bilingual, Australian*	Focus: Phrases that give examples
TOPIC 5 Getting to Know You	Unit 9	Analyze characters	*calm, nervous, daring, shy, rude, thoughtful, confident, friendly*	Write a comparative report
	Unit 10	Understand types of conflict	*fit, strong, studious, proud, brave, patient, busy, generous*	Focus: Phrases that show contrast
TOPIC 6 Finding Adventure	Unit 11	Make a value judgment	*Amazon jungle, Mt. Everest, pyramid, culture, currency, go kayaking, rock climbing, national park*	Write a research report
	Unit 12	Understand a pie chart	*go to Mars, exciting, Antarctica, population, mountain range, glacier, the bottom of the ocean, determined*	Focus: Synonyms